THE ASTROLOGY OF

2019

BIRTHING
YOUR INNER CHILD

Photography by Alex Richardson

Gahl Sasson is an established author and has been teaching workshops on Storytelling, Kabbalah, Astrology, and Mysticism around the globe for over 20 years.

His first book, *A Wish Can Change Your Life*, has been translated into over eight languages and is endorsed by HH the 14th Dalai Lama. His latest work, *Cosmic Navigator*, is the essential reference guide to understanding your astrological makeup.

He is a contributor to the Huffington Post, and Astrology.com, and has been named by W Magazine as one of "Los Angeles' Best Astrologer." Gahl was also chosen by Asia Spa Magazine as one of the 10 leading health practitioners in the world. He is a guest lecturer at USC, Tel Aviv University, and teaches at Esalen, Omega Institute, University of Judaism, and the Open Center in NYC. He has appeared on CNN, ABC News, KTLA-TV Los Angeles to name a few. In 2017 his academic article, *Symbolic Meaning of Names in the Bible* was published by the Journal of Storytelling, Self, & Society. He currently resides in Los Angeles, but gives seminars and workshops regularly in USA, Argentina, Canada, Mexico, Russia, Lithuania, UK, Germany, Hong Kong, Spain, Belgium, Singapore, Turkey, Israel, Bulgaria, and Switzerland. His web site is www.CosmicNavigator.com

*Special thanks to Kibea Publishing
for designing the book
and to Michael Davis' editing skills.
Photography: Alex Richardson*

GAHL EDEN SASSON

THE ASTROLOGY OF 2019

WELCOME TO YOUR COSMIC YEARLY GUIDE FOR THE WIS-
DOM OF THE STARS. 2019 is the year you give birth to your inner
child. Conception took place in 2017; gestation during 2018; and in
the year 2019, you will give light to your true self. You will be asked
to be nurturing and practice compassion towards your new self and,
just as a mother must love her newborn unconditionally, so must you
raise yourself with loving-kindness.

Since in 2019 you are reborn, you will need to give yourself a
spiritual name. You don't need a guru or a sage to do that for you.
You don't even have to tell anyone your self-given name. Your
spiritual name should be private and used whenever you need help
from your guides or the universe. Make sure your spiritual name has
a meaning and that the story of the name reflects your life mission.

2019 is an interesting year. Many planets return home to their signs and therefore they will be able to shine without obstruction. It is like planting native plants in their place of origin. We already have Neptune in Pisces since 2012, Saturn in Capricorn since December 2017, and from November 2018, Jupiter in Sagittarius. This is actually very good. The transit of Jupiter, the planet of fortune and benevolence, in Sagittarius is especially auspicious. This aspect brings luck, synchronicities, flow, expansion, as well as opportunities in travel and education.

In 2019 you will experience a great deal of oppositions. On one side, 2019 asks us to focus on family, parenting, and building a nest. On the other side, it bids us to pay extra attention to our career and professional life. 2019 also pits luck, opportunities, and fortune against delays, challenges, and discipline. Is 2019 a lucky year that jinxed? A good or bad year? You should get used to feeling great and terrible at the same time. We can call 2019 a manic-depressive year and we will have to learn how to find balance and integrate oppositions.

Remember, you are magic and astrology is your wand. Magic is defined as a transformative intention bound by space and time. Your soul is a transformative intention. In many mystical traditions, your soul is viewed as a thought of the creator. The binding of space and time that allows your soul's transformation and, therefore, the magic, is your time and place of birth. This book can help you use the magic wand of astrology to navigate the year.

I wish you, your loved ones, friends, and pets a happy and healthy year full of abundance, creativity, love, and adventures. It is a wonderful thing to be a human and we are fortunate to have reincarnated during this era at the dawning of the Age of Aquarius, the age of awareness.

I hope to see you in person in one of my lectures around the globe.

Gahl
Alacati, Turkey

GENERAL GUIDELINES

MERCURY RETROGRADES

March 5–28:	Mercury retrogrades in Pisces:
July 7–31:	Mercury retrogrades in Leo (until July 19) and then moves to Cancer.
October 31 – November 20:	Mercury retrogrades in Scorpio.

 ## SOLAR AND LUNAR ECLIPSES

January 5–6:	Partial Solar Eclipse in Capricorn.
January 20–21:	Total Lunar Eclipse Leo/Cancer cusp.
July 2:	Total Solar Eclipse Cancer.
July 16–17:	Partial Lunar Eclipse Capricorn.
December 26:	Annular Solar Eclipse Capricorn.

part one

Introduction
to Cosmic Trends

Astrology – Mother of Sciences and Religions

Astrology is dubbed the mother of sciences. The act of measuring, calculating, and tracking the heavenly bodies helped transform the early stargazers into prototype empirical scientists. It is believed that the scientific fields of geometry and algebra developed to better understand and predict the cycles of the planets. It is not surprising that Kepler, the father of astronomy, was an avid astrologer. But astrology is not only the mother of sciences. She is also the mother of science's older sister, religion.

I believe that when our hominid ancestors started walking on two legs, their field of vision changed, shifting their focus from the earth to the skies. In addition, due to climate changes, hominid environment morphed from thick jungles where the skies were covered by jungle canopy, into open fields, savannas where the starry skies could be viewed with no obstruction. Our ancestors were exposed to the vastness of space and could bear witness in awe to the movement of the planets through the backdrop of the fixed stars, the constellations. First there was astrology, then came religion to give ritualistic stories to the movement of the cosmic bodies and the seasons.

Astrology's DNA is found in countless religions and traditions around the globe. The Mayans, Aztecs, druids, and ancient Egyptians aligned their pyramids or rock formations in reference to cosmology. In Islam, the Ramadan, a commemoration of the first revelation of the *Koran*, is celebrated according to the moon and always falls on the 9th lunar month. The Buddhists celebrate the Buddha's birthday on the full moon in the month of *Vesakha* (which usually falls on the full moon in Taurus). Christmas is a Christianized celebration of the pagan winter solstice, placing Jesus' birthday on the solstice along with Mithras, Attis, Apollo, Artemis, and Horus to name a few. Passover is the celebration of equinox (which falls on the first full moon after the equinox). Easter is celebrated according to an astrological formula: the first Sunday (the day of the Sun) after the first full moon (sun-moon opposition) after the spring equinox (the first day of Aries). The Chinese, Islamic, Tibetan, and Jewish New Years, fall on a new moon. The Persian New Year, *Nawruz*, is celebrated on the spring equinox, the first day of Aries, which is also the astrological New Year's. Halloween is celebrated during Scorpio, the sign of death. Earth day is commemorated during Taurus, a fixed earth sign, that associated with Mother Nature. Labor Day (in the US) is celebrated during Virgo, the sign of work and service. The International Cat Day is celebrated August 8, the 8 of the 8, double happiness, smack in the middle of Leo, the feline sign. Your birthday, too, is an astrological holiday. It is the day when your natal sun is conjunct the transiting sun. It is a day when you are exposed to two suns. No wonder that on your birthday you are emotional, overly sensitive, and need of extra attention and gifts.

Astrology is not a fortune-telling art. She was created and still functions as a tool to help us survive. I trace the origin of astrology to a woman or a group of women in our early human evolution that realized the connection between intercourse and pregnancy. There was a period in our evolution when the main cause of death for women was giving birth. Because of bipedalism, the combination of a shift in the pelvis and the growing diameter of the fetus' head, childbearing became a deadly activity. There had to be a woman, arguably, the most important scientist in human history, who discovered that intercourse leads to pregnancy and that somehow these two are linked to the menstruation cycles. Now all she needed was to find a way to trace the cycles and measure them to determine when intercourse will not result in pregnancy. She needed a contraceptive. Looking up at the Moon gave her what she sought, a cosmic clock. This intuitive woman, the first astrologer, managed to find a connection between the moon cycles and ovulation: as above so below, the birth of astrology. The wisdom of the stars, astrology, helped us survive as a species and ensured our ability to overcome the death that overshadowed birth.

Numerology of 2019

In numerology, 2018 adds up to 11, a master number, as well as to 2, the number of pregnancy. One can argue that 2018 was a prenatal year, a painful year for many of us, a difficult pregnancy for some. A great deal of morning sickness and confusion took place in 2018 especially around the eclipses, January, February, July, and August. 2019 is the year when the baby is being born. I cannot promise you an easy birthing. It might be a long labor. You will have to breathe deeply and maybe scream a little, but rest assured, you are pregnant with your Self.

In 2019, you will have to exercise a great deal of discipline and endurance. The reason is that the sign Capricorn steals the cosmic stage. This year we have Pluto, Saturn, and some of the eclipses all converging in Capricorn, a sign that favors focus and strategy. In December, Jupiter will also join the Capricorn gang. The combination of Saturn (ruler of discipline and restriction) in Capricorn (sign of maturity and cautiousness) with Jupiter (luck and expansion) in Sagittarius (sign of opportunities and optimism), means that 2019 is a roller coaster. It orbits around words like inflation, devaluation, changing interest rates, savings, bubbles bursting, and a great deal of ups and downs both emotionally and financially.

Numbers are Stories Quantified

In many languages, the word for "number" shares the same etymology as the word for "story." In English, I am asked for my account's password and, at the same time, I can tell my friend an *account* of what has transpired at work. In Spanish, I can ask for *la cuenta*, my bill, but also tell a story *contar un cuento*. In Hebrew, a number is called *Mispar* (root SPR) and a story is *Sipur* (same root). These ancient truths embedded in many languages show that numbers are not only for counting quantities but also for describing qualities. They tell stories. This is of course the foundation of numerology.

2019 (2+0+1+9=12) adds up to the number 12. Usually in numerology, we reduce numbers above 9. For example, 2017 adds to 10 and then we reduce 10 to 1 since 1+0 is 1. Therefore, 12 is reduced to the number 3. While 12 is not a master number (as was the case in the year 2018), it is still a vessel for powerful symbolism.

 The Twelve

And there appeared a great wonder in heaven; clothed with the sun, and the moon under her feet, and upon her head a crown of twelve stars. And she being with child cried, travailing in birth...

— *New Testament, Revelation* 12

Before we examine the meaning of the number 3, let us take a deeper look at 12 and how it mirrors the cosmic atmosphere of the year 2019. In many different traditions, the number 12 tells the story of completion, wholesomeness, a circle closed, the creation of a community. From Western astrology to Vedic and Chinese astrology, the 12 months of the year are represented by 12 signs. The Sumerians, who first conceived of the zodiac wheel, were also the inventors of maps and the wheel. They considered 12 a sacred number. Their bequest was the division of the sky into 12 constellations we still use today. For them, there was a completion, an entirety of creation between Aries and Pisces. Life as a whole can be described by these 12 architypes. The bible, which was influenced by Mesopotamian philosophies and culture, gave Jacob 12 children, which later became the 12 tribes. For this reason, the high priest in the temple of Jerusalem wore the *Ephod,* a vest adorned with 12 stones, which he used for divination. Jesus, a poor mystic preaching in an occupied land, had 12 apostles that within 3 centuries managed to conquer the Roman empire with a message of love and passive resistance. In Eumenides' play, *Aeschylus,* Athena, the goddess of wisdom, creates a system of law with 12 jurors. In Buddhism, there are 12 *Nidanas* in the outer rim of the Wheel of Becoming, which represent the entire process of cause and effect. In Islam, there were 12 Imams that succeeded Muhammad. In the Arthurian saga, King Arthur had 12 knights that sat around the round table. And of course, one must never forget, the 12 Olympian gods and goddesses.

From all these world-wide mythological examples, there are a few themes that repeat: a circle composed of signs, constellations, knights, imams, apostles, tribes, animals, and gods. 12 represents the wheel, with no beginning and no end, humankind's greatest invention that facilitates movement and change. From the Buddhist wheel of cause and effect to the zodiac (meaning "wheel of animals") and the wheel of fortune, 12 represents motion and fluidity. *Mazal,* Hebrew for sign or constellation, comes from the root NZL, "to flow." If you want to make the best of 2019 and be true to its numerological attributes, you need to flow, to let go, to generate movement and bring mutability into your life. Don't get stuck or be too stubborn. Don't fixate! As Mother Mary whispered: let it be, just let it be.

However, there is an active aspect to 12 as well. Knights are sent on a mission to retrieve the Holy Grail, Jesus sent his apostles to spread the good word, and the 12 tribes were sent to conquer the land promised to Jacob and his grandad, Abraham. This year, you need your gang, your community, your knights, and apostles. You need a platform, a fraternity, a group of friends or colleagues that can help you conquer your holy land, or aid in your quest.

 The Trinity

"Do not train a child to learn by force or harshness; but direct them to it by what amuses their minds, so that you may be better able to discover with accuracy the peculiar bent of the genius of each."

Plato

The number 3 is represented in sacred geometry by the tringle, the first enclosed shape on a two-dimensional plane. In Kabbalah, the 3rd sphere in the Tree of Life is called *Binah*, Understanding, and it is associated with the *Shekinah*, the divine feminine. 3 helps us navigate the time space continuum. Time: past, present, future. Space: length, width, and height. In numerology, 3 represents the child, the product of the union of 1 and 2. You can see the underlining story of the great Mother giving birth to the Child. In Christianity, 3 is the Trinity and in Hindu tradition it is the 3 godhead of Brahma (creator), Vishnu (sustainer) and Shiva (destroyer). There are also 3 pillars in the Tree of Life supporting creation. In astrology, there are 3 modalities: Cardinal signs (Aries, Cancer, Libra, Capricorn); Fixed signs (Leo, Scorpio, Aquarius, Taurus); and Mutable signs (Sagittarius, Pisces, Gemini, Virgo). And of course, there are 3 fates that give, measure, and cut the thread of life.

The enduring transcultural symbolism of 3 gives 2019 the power of construction and creation. The child is procreation, the ability to generate life and creativity. The true Trinity is the story of the Father, the Mother and the holy Child. This year, you can connect to the Trinity in your own mythology. Who is your true father (could be biological and could be spiritual); who is your mother, your Shekinah? Also, who is your child? It could be an idea, a business, a mission, or a creation.

Plato's quote above holds a powerful message for next year. 2019 is not solely about giving birth to a child or a creative product, but it is also about reconnecting with and raising your inner child. You might have been subject to harsh education when you were younger and many of your passions and talents might have been suppressed by ignorant educators. 2019 is the best year to reeducate your inner child and reconnect to the "accuracy the peculiar bent of the genius of each."

2019 also affords you the ability to fix your Trinity, to make peace as well as heal your Trinity of father-mother-you. Even if your parents are not alive, you are still influenced by ancestral karma that runs down the generations through your genes, attitudes, education, and traits. This year you will find opportunities to remove these blocks. Especially, as you will see below, during the eclipses in January, July, and December.

New Year's Resolution –
When and Why

Year after year, in my classes around the globe, I repeat the concept that New Year's is the only truly scared holiday that appeals to all of humanity regardless of race, culture, and religion. New Year's celebration is the only absolute holy day. While Christmas, Ramadan, Hanukkah, Vesak, Utsava, Yule, etc., are culturally relative holy days—that is, conditioned, and therefore limited, by faith, religion, or location—New Year's is the only holiday celebrated by atheists and believers alike

In Istanbul, which for the last 500 years has been predominately Muslim, on New Year's, the streets are glowing with bright festive lights and the trees are adorned with LCD lights. My family and friends in Israel, mainly Jewish, also celebrate New Year's and adhere to the traditional midnight countdown. My friends in Los Angeles, where I live, mainly Christians or atheists, also celebrate the arrival of the new year. My colleagues in Hong Kong, mostly Buddhist, send each other Happy New Year greetings. What a wonderful holiday! It is a true Earth celebration from New Zealand to Norway, Japan to the US, Finland to Argentina. No matter where you are on the planet, you, your friends and family, your cellphone and computers will switch from 2018 to 2019 with a big bang and a splash. Arguably, New Year's is the most popular celebration on the planet. How glorious it is that New Year's is sealed with a countdown 10,9,8...1 and then a kiss! Practically a numerological ritual, you invoke all the 10 archetypes and then you join lips with a kiss and a hug. Without noticing, humankind created a celebration of commonality. It reminds me of the words of Shakespeare: "What a piece of work is a man, how noble in reason, how infinite in faculties, in form and moving how express and admirable, in action how like an angel, in apprehension how like a god!"

Janus, the Roman god of portals and the namesake of January, is a perfect symbol for New Year's. Like the god's image, we spend New Year's splitting our consciousness between reviewing what we experienced in 2018 and projecting and envisioning what we wish to experience in 2019. Since over 7 billion people initiate the year in January 1, even if it never was astrologically significant, it becomes an energetic vortex from all the attention it receives. Therefore, on January 1, do many symbolic acts that represent what you want to focus on in 2019. The first day of the year, as well as the first week of January, is the overture of the year ahead when you play the melodies of what you wish to hear the next 12 months. For example, if your new year resolution relates to love, then do something that represents relationships on the first day or week of the year. If it is a new diet, then eat healthy on January 1.

Recent studies demonstrate that less than 10% succeeded in manifesting their New Year's resolutions. I believe you can increase the success rate by starting in the right time. Like a surfer, you need to catch the right wave and paddle strong before the wave reaches you. While it is possible to decide what you want to accomplish in 2019 on New Year's, it is not the best time to start the manifestation. Here are a few dates that would be best to start the working on making your resolution come true:

- Partial Solar eclipse in Capricorn January 5/6. If your resolution is for a long-term goal, something you will need a great deal of time, discipline, and focus to manifest, this is a good time.

- Exalted Moon in Taurus trine Sun January 16. It is a good time to start a New Year's resolution that deals with emotions, finance, career, or art.

- Chinese New Year, New Moon in Aquarius on February 4/5, Earth Boar. The Boar or Pig New Year is a good time to start a project that involves communication, writing (blog, books, or business plans), community, friends, generosity, leisure, meditation, destressing, technology, and renewal.

- Valentine's trine Moon Sun in air signs, February 14/15. This day favors resolutions involving forming a company, connecting to friends or clubs, government, or relationships in general.

- March 20, Equinox — Astrological New Year. Traditionally the first day of Aries is a good time to start new projects, but this year it falls under Mercury Retrograde so take extra care.

 The Year of the Earth Pig – Yin

The Boar or Pig is the 12th sign in the Chinese Zodiac. If you were born in 1923, 1935, 1947, 1959, 1971, 1983, 1995, 2007, or 2019, then you are a member of the pig clan. You are in good company. Other famous pigs are: Emma Thompson, Arnold Schwarzenegger,

Hillary Rodham Clinton, Woody Allen, Julie Andrews, Ronald Reagan, Mahalia Jackson, King Henry VIII, Alfred Hitchcock, Lucille Ball, and Ernest Hemingway to name a few. The year of the pig starts February 4, 2019 and lasts until January 25, 2020.

The pig is associated with the piggy bank. Small deposits in a savings account that cannot be opened for a while is recommended. It is best not to spend too much and to avoid gluttony, which will be hard when Jupiter is in Sagittarius, an overly generous sign. Pigs tend to be wealthy and that means that you have a chance to improve your finance this year. The pigs like entertainment and therefore there could be some changes in the way we entertain ourselves (movies, music, games, theater) and how entertainment is available to us.

This year is a highly social year. It is recommended that you surround yourself with friends and family and not stay alone or in solitude. Avoid procuring debt (karmic and/or financial). The year is also marked by an ability to share and exchange services and benefits. It is a good year for barter as well as sharing economies. The pig year is great for exercising giving and receiving. However, the year can be rather hedonistic and lustful. In romance, be careful of extramarital affairs or short, hot, passionate relationships that cannot outlast their lust. Be careful of overindulgence. Pigs, unlike the roosters, do not like to be in the center of attention and do not waste time or energy promoting themselves, however, they do what they say. Very pragmatic and practical sign which fits well with the 2019 cluster of planets in Capricorn, the grounded earth sign.

The year of the pig is also the year of the boar and in many traditions, the boar represents defensiveness, protectionism, and warlike tendencies. With all the trade wars and the rise of nationalism, one can only hope that 2019 is a piglet year rather than a boar.

I have asked my dear colleague Deborah Kagan who is a Feng Shui master as well as an author, speaker, and Mojo Recovery Specialists to write share her thoughts about the qualities of the Year of the Pig:

2019's Year of the Pig continues the two-year Earth Element cycle that the Dog ushered in for us in 2018. The Earth Pig is sensible and thoughtful. Practical steps continue to be the name of the game. Social interactions and integrity motivate this animal/element combo therefore, this is the year to try anything because succeeding against vast odds is possible, if you come from your heart.

The Pig is very popular and sought after because it seeks universal harmony. Pig's put their heart and soul into whatever it is they do, which makes them incredibly magnetic. People become enchanted with their fortitude and goodwill usually wanting to join forces with them. The Pig is never at a loss for support on projects. Of course, there's always a yin to each yang. In the case of the Pig, they can suffer from being overgenerous, overoptimistic and having a difficult time saying no. The message of the Earth Pig is to dive into your life with eyes wide open and know that you can create your hearts desires this year with an abundance of outer encouragement.

2019 is also a year of potential muddy thinking. The Earth Pig luxuriates on a stage that is inherently made of water (Pig's natural element). This elemental dance of earth and water causes things that do not easily coexist to come to the surface. Fear not (the Pig happily trots into the unknown) because this elemental friction assists you in getting creative to make your visions reality.

One of the best ways to do that is by sharing more of yourself through gatherings. All sorts of them... parties, conventions, clubs, associations. Any chance you get to be amongst a group of people— take it. The Pig loves being around others because they can make connections. And connecting people from different sides is one of the things the Pig does best. But be cautious of the Pig's desire for indulgence. Yes, our sweet little Piggy can be just that. So with all your getting out and about, do be aware of your gluttonous urges in all aspects of life this year.

The Pig is the most blessed sign of the Chinese zodiac. Being under its influence this year brings infinite blessings to you and your life. What are your dreams? What are you ready to bring to the world? Everything is available to you this year. Shine your light for the liberation of all.

Eclipses – One Extra Lunation in 2019

As was the case with 2018, 2019 boasts 5 eclipses instead of the regular four. This means that in 2019 things are moving turbo fast, especially since in this year, unlike in 2018, we do not have Mars and Venus retrogrades to slow down the pace.

It is through a remarkable synchronicity that the solar disk is 400 times bigger but also 400 times farther than the moon. For this reason, their surfaces appear to have the same size when viewed from earth. Perhaps this is a heavenly reminder that the feminine (moon) and masculine (sun) are equal. It is a metaphor, a cosmic poem, showing us that reception (moon) is just as important as action (sun) to achieve our goals. This synchronicity makes the eclipses possible since, from the viewpoint of an earthling, the moon and sun's disks can cover each other like a perfectly-tailored garment.

Eclipses are wild-cards. They are unpredictable and tend to accelerate and amplify whatever process is currently happening in your life. That is the reason many people experienced such an intense period during the months of January/February and July/August of 2018. The eclipses in 2017 and 2018 were in Leo and Aquarius. However, since November 2018, the North Node, also known as the Head of the Dragon, moved into Cancer, which means that until June 2020, the karmic lessons as manifested through the eclipses are shifting to the axis of Cancer/Capricorn. Gone are the lessons of Leo and hereafter are the lessons of Cancer.

THE DEVIL. Since Capricorn is the opposite sign of Cancer, this earth-bender sign will help teach us the lessons of Cancer. Therefore, we must be attentive to the lessons of both signs. Cancer teaches us about family, mothering, security, home, real-estate, emotions, compassion, birthing, and parenting but might also force us to deal with issues such as attachment, guilt, and shame. Capricorn's lessons are focused on career, ambition, father figures, discipline, plan, strategy, and patience but can also cause us to confront issues such as fears, rigidity, greed, ego, and pessimism. Capricorn contains our collective fears, such as the boogey man, demons, and the Devil (which is the Tarot card of Capricorn). The reason for the association of fear with Capricorn is via the fear of survival. Capricorn takes place in the Northern Hemisphere during the harsh winter months when food is scarce. Cancer, on the other hand is the sign of motherhood, compassion, and unconditional love and is considered the antidote for Capricorn's fears. Together, Cancer and

Capricorn create a powerful axis of the Holy Grail (Capricorn) and Holy Water (Cancer). These are the mythologies the eclipses are bringing into the limelight in 2019 and 2020.

This series of eclipses in the axis of Cancer and Capricorn happened in 1999/2000 and in 1981/1982. Remember that astrology takes us to the past so we can better understand the present and helps design our future. Try to recall what happened to you in those years (mistakes or good choices) so you can navigate and create the year ahead in a better way.

To better understand how the eclipses would work for you in 2019 and 2020, look at whatever transpired around July 13, 2018. That was the first of the eclipse series in Cancer and Capricorn. Let's take a look at what happened around middle July in the news. Right on July 13, Special Counsel, Robert S. Mueller III, indicted twelve Russian GRU (military intelligence) officers for cyber-attacks and attempting to interfere in the US elections. Remember, the Russian's meddling in US elections was/is arguably, after September 11, one of the most devastating attacks on American soil. The US is of course a Cancer (born July 4) and the last time the eclipses were in Cancer was 2000 and 2001, right when the 9-11 attacks took place.

Three days later, like a reverberation or a ripple, at the Hall of Mirrors in the Presidential Palace in Helsinki, with no prior precedence, the president of the US sided with an ex-KGB agent and head of a hostile state against his own security services. Eclipses, indeed, quicken processes. Eclipses weave stories and we can expect that this saga will continue to unfold and grab the news cycles again when the eclipses in Cancer return (January and July of 2019).

Around the eclipses in January, July, and December of 2019, you will experience many more meaningful coincidences and serendipities that can serve as omens or signs from the universe. Eclipses also are known to be storytellers and generators of synchronicities.

The eclipses occur on specific days, but their sphere of influence or radiation can be felt a week before and after. However, their stories unfold for sometimes as long as six months.

Below you will find a list of the eclipses' dates as well as what is called their Sabian symbol. The Sabian symbols were conceived in 1925 by clairvoyant Elsie Wheeler and provide each degree in the zodiac with a specific image or story that can help navigate the synchronicities of the eclipse. Some of the images will appear random or even strange, but I find them helpful. I also listed the areas where the eclipses can be seen, which are usually the places that experience more of a lunation's influence.

Remember, solar eclipses are a conjunction of the sun and the moon. Action and reception are linked, and both are needed simultaneously. Lunar eclipses are an opposition between the sun (action) and the moon (reception) and therefore ask us to balance between the need to act and the need to be patient and learn to receive.

January 5–6: *Partial Solar Eclipse in Capricorn.* New Moon in Capricorn. A great day to start the New Year's Resolution. Sabian symbol: School grounds filled with boys and girls in gymnasium suits. Visible: East Asia, Pacific. Focus on career, your ambition, discipline, making plans, and dealing with father figures or bosses.

January 20–21: *Total Lunar Eclipse Leo/Cancer cusp.* This full moon takes place right on the border between Cancer and Leo. Sabian symbol: Under emotional stress, blood rushes to a man's head. Visible: Europe, Asia, Africa, North America, South America, Pacific, Atlantic, Indian Ocean, Arctic. Focus on home and family

versus career, children versus friends or community. Action in career can help receive some change in your home and family.

July 2: *Total Solar Eclipse Cancer.* This new moon marks a new beginning in your family life or emotional space. Sabian symbol: A clown making grimaces. Visible: Some regions in the Pacific and in South America. Focus on family, motherhood, parenting, home, and real-estate.

July 16–17: *Partial Lunar Eclipse Capricorn.* Full moon in Capricorn, pitting career against home and family, mother figures versus father figures. This eclipse can be extra sensitive. Sabian symbol: An oriental rug dealer. Visible: Much of Europe, much of Asia, Australia, Africa, South/East of North America, South America, Pacific, Atlantic, Indian Ocean. Focus on balancing worldly ambition, and emotional needs. Action in your family can help receive change in career.

December 26: *Annular Solar Eclipse Capricorn.* New Moon in Capricorn, a good time to think about your next New Year's resolution. Something new coming into your career. Sabian Symbol: Indians rowing a canoe and dancing a war dance. Visible: Saudi Arabia, Oman, India, Sri Lanka, Singapore, Malaysia, Indonesia, South Philippines. Focus on structure, discipline, and making long term plans.

About a week before and after the dates of the eclipses, you might feel emotional, reactive, and sensitive, especially since, as you saw above, the eclipses take place in Cancer (the sign of emotion) and

Capricorn (the sign that rules fear). There is a reason why the mythical werewolves transform into beasts during the lunation. During the eclipses, we become more instinctual and less governed by reason. Our animalistic side takes control of us and the eclipses expose our wounded inner child.

Be strong in those periods for yourself as well as for the people around you. Knowing these astrological trends make you more responsible. You are reading these pages so that you can become a lighthouse for others as well as for yourself. It is recommended to spend time near water during the eclipses. If your birthday falls close to the dates of the eclipse it means that the next 12 months will be full of events.

 ## Mother of Dragons

I want to make a little pause and further explain the concepts of the lunar nodes that are not planets but mathematical points accounting for the relationship between the paths of the Sun (father), Moon (Mother), and Earth (our lives). The North Node, as we mentioned before, is also called the Head of the Dragon and represents what our soul desires, what we have to learn in order for us to soar up high like angels. The South Node, on the other hand, is called the Tail of the Dragon, and it symbolizes aspects of life we already explored in past lives and therefore need to let go, like sandbags that keep the balloon from rising. Imagine you are flying from your country to a new exotic place. The tail of your dragon points back towards your native homeland while the head of the dragon is looking forward to new experiences in a foreign land.

What is a dragon and why it is venerated in different mythologies around the globe? Perhaps it is a genetic memory we carry in our mammalian DNA of the great dinosaurs? Perchance it is because the mythical beast is the combination of a reptile that crawls in the ground and an eagle that soars above? Maybe the dragon's spiritual powers come from the fact that it is a manifestation of the ancient alchemical axiom: as above, so below.

As we saw earlier, from mid-November 2018, the Head of the Dragon moved from Leo to Cancer, the sign of the Mother, and with this shift our karma or soul lessons also changed. In the next two years, as the Head of the Dragon is looking at the Lady of Avalon, or the Mother of Dragons, for guidance, we need to focus on compassion, learn unconditional love, acceptance, healing, and emoting. The North Node in Cancer is asking us to connect to family and home. Since the Tail of the Dragon is in Capricorn, 2019 is the year when we are asked to let go of Capricorn's energy in general, but specifically its dark side: fears for survival, greed, ignorance, nationalism, over-ambition, and achieving success at all costs.

Saturn, Planet of Karma in Capricorn

From December 20, 2017 until March 22, 2020, Saturn, the planet of karma, travels through Capricorn. 2019 falls right in the middle of Saturn's transit in the mountainous road of Capricorn. Saturn, in the Kabbalistic Tree of Life, is associated with the Sphere Binah, "Understanding," and wherever Saturn travels, he teaches us what we must understand in order to grow. Kabbalah suggests that Saturn is the rectifier, Tikkun, the celestial contractor that helps fix the sign or house where he is located. Saturn is the planet that helps us grow through crisis.

Since Saturn enjoys traveling in Capricorn, we will all benefit from this transit as long as we are focused, disciplined, and serious. Saturn in Capricorn can help with our ambition, concentration, and career. Saturn in Capricorn is practical and pragmatic but tends to be conservative and somewhat cautious. For this reason, Saturn in Capricorn, especially with Pluto also being in Capricorn, can bring our collective fears to the surface.

Unfortunately, the dark side of Saturn in Capricorn, the conservative sign, is the rise of the alternative right on the political spectrum as well as nationalism and racism. What is nationalism? It is a collective ego of an imagined group of people. Nationalists like to point out that they are proud of their country or tribe. But what makes a country? A set a myths and stories. We now know that people who think of themselves as "pure blooded" Polish or American are actually far from that. With the help of DNA analysis, to the embarrassment of many so-called nationalists, it is possible to show how mixed their genes are. We must accept that in the Age of Aquarius, the goal is oneness and not separation. Saturn in Capricorn can help us galvanize and crystalize our potential and manifest it. However, he can also cause our fears and demons to take over our lives.

Capricorn is not an easy sign. In late 2008, when Pluto moved into Capricorn, we experienced the Great Recession. How can we work better with Capricorn? First, we must overcome the fear of survival. We must acknowledge that life is not made of scarce resources, and that the more we give the more we have. Capricorn can help us make solid plans and galvanize our gifts, transforming inner wealth into outer abundance. Capricorn is a sign that can help us manifest, making things happen in space-time existence. Saturn is the taskmaster, the builder of walls. When Saturn was in Capricorn, the Berlin Wall was built. The next time Saturn was in Capricorn the Berlin Wall fell along with the Soviet Empire and the Iron Curtain. It is karmically comical to hear people like Donald Trump raving seriously about building another wall.

To learn how Saturn in Capricorn affected your life in the past, look at the dates below. It can help you understand what Saturn wants to teach you the next two years.

Saturn in Capricorn: February to June 1988 and November 1988 to February 1991; January 1959 to January 1962.

If you are born between January 1 to 12, you will experience the pressure of Saturn stronger as Saturn will transit over your sun this year. This can manifest as extra pressure, or father figure issues as well as higher expectations coming from bosses and older people. Your ability to stay calm will be tested, but you will find yourself maturing and discovering your true purpose. This happens once every 28-30 years. It is an injection of maturity and identity.

Taurus and Virgo, being fellow earth signs can benefit from the transit of Saturn in Capricorn. They will get help constructing new things in their lives as well as help in their careers. Cancers, however, might feel some difficulties with people of authority or a general feeling of opposition as Saturn will oppose their sun and self-expression. Aries and Libra will have a square forming with Saturn, thus some fights and discord with father figures or bosses. For Capricorns it is an opportunity to rebrand themselves and start a new path in life.

The 2019 Paradox

Paradoxes are powerful tools to help us see the folly of duality and leap from logic to enlightenment. The famous Zen *Koans* are non-sensical and paradoxical stanzas (an example below) that help our minds overcome right and wrong, true and false, yes and no and leap into oneness.

2019 is such a koan year that presents us with an unsolvable paradox. On the one hand, is the stellium (cluster of planets) in Capricorn, led by Saturn, Pluto, most of the eclipses, and from December 2019, Jupiter as well. On the other hand, we have the South Node in Capricorn. Why is it a paradox? Saturn is the great teacher and his location indicates where we must focus our intention and attention in order to grow. Since Saturn is the ruler of Capricorn and he is now in Capricorn, he wants us to learn the lessons of his sign: persistence, endurance, discipline, patience, planning, strategy, career, and ambition. As we saw earlier, the South Node's sign shows us what energy we must let go in order to grow. This means that we must connect and disconnect to Capricorn at the same time.

What then should we do? We must do both. We must overcome duality, the either/or; yes/no; 0/1 mentality. We must integrate. We must be disciplined (Capricorn) with our compassion. We must use our ambition (Capricorn) to improve our home life (Cancer). Remember, not choices but integration and balance can help us this year. For every sign, I will state the paradox for the year in Part II. Here is a beautiful example of a Koan to inspire your 2019 integration:

Two monks were in a heated argument about the temple flags flapping in the wind. The first said: "The flag moves." The other replied,

"No, the wind moves." They could not agree until Hui-neng, the master, appeared and said: *"It is not the flag that moves. It is not the wind that moves. It is your mind that moves."*

 **Jupiter in Sagittarius**

While ancient astrologers looked at the location of Saturn in a chart to determine "bad" news, they searched for Jupiter to deliver the "good" tidings. Saturn teaches with the stick while Jupiter illuminates with carrots. Jupiter is the grand benevolent planet and presents us with opportunities to expand our horizons. After all, he is the biggest planet in our solar system and is constantly expanding.

Once in twelve years, Jupiter returns home to Sagittarius, the sign he rules. This is great news regardless whether you are a Sagittarius. When Jupiter is planted in his native archetypal soil, he blooms and grows faster and better than in any other location.

Jupiter moved into Sagittarius November 8, 2018 and will be in his sign until December 2/3, 2019. Jupiter will then transit into Capricorn, preparing the great Capricorn showdown of 2020.

Jupiter in Sagittarius can bring success and opportunities in education, travel, mass media, publishing, improved relationships with in-laws, philosophy, generosity, and tolerance. Jupiter's tarot card is called Fortune, and when Jupiter is in Sagittarius, the wheel of fortune is on your side. In other words, lady luck is smiling at you.

Jupiter's transit into Sagittarius is great news for Sagittarians or people with Sagittarius rising. It means that your path is clear and there are no traffic police, you can drive full speed ahead. Other signs that can benefit from Jupiter in Sagittarius are Leo and Aries, the other members of the fire nation. Gemini, the opposite sign must be extra careful of excesses and being over-the-top.

According to the *Astrology of Becoming*, (see my book, *Cosmic Navigator*) even if you are not a Sagittarius, you can still benefit from Jupiter's gifts in 2019 by "becoming" a Sagittarius. You can embody the positive qualities of our Centaurian friends, thus attracting the gifts that Jupiter bestows on the sign throughout 2019. How to become a Sagittarius? I always consider the Sagittarian to be the Indian Jones of the zodiac. You need to be optimistic, adventurous, connect to education and foreign cultures, and never give up. Be authentic and truthful. Encourage luck. How? When you get a great parking spot against all odds, say out loud "Wow, I am lucky!" However, be careful of not being overly optimistic, or spreading yourself over too many projects or commitments.

Look back at the last times Jupiter has been in Sagittarius to see how this cycle worked personally with you: November 24, 2006 to December 18, 2007; December 9, 1994 to January 3, 1996; December 25, 1982 to January 19, 1984; September 11, 1971 to February 6, 1972; July 24, 1972 to Sep 25, 1972; June 9, 1960 to October 25, 1960; and February 10, 1959 to April 24, 1959.

From December 2/3, in the last few weeks of 2019, Jupiter transits into Capricorn and our goat friends will experience an overload of planets in their sign. Jupiter, Pluto, Saturn, and the eclipses all come together in Capricorn, giving us a great opportunity to focus and manifest our career and professional life.

This year, Jupiter retrogrades from April 10 to August 12. At that time, you might feel some delays and challenges in receiving help from the universe. It is especially tough in July when the eclipses and Mercury Retrograde add backward motion to Jupiter. After August 12, projects that were delayed from April will open up and flow much more.

Venus' Love Affairs

Venus, the archetype of love, relationships, art, beauty and justice is not retrograding this year, which is great for relationships of all kind. In the sections of the signs you will find when she is visiting your sign and bestowing you with her grace.

Three aspects I wanted to mention now that can help you connect to Venus. The first is her conjunction with Jupiter on January 22/23 and November 24/25. These aspects are pure luck and benevolence. The wheel of fortune is spinning in our favor. It is a time of expansion and opportunities in art, love, and finance.

Between August 23–26 Venus will meet her secret lover, Mars, the archetype of passion and action, and they will make celestial love. We will all feel this passionate reunion of the masculine and feminine archetypes in many facets of our lives. In 2018 they did not meet, which is very rare. Maybe they had a falling out or a nasty breakup, but in 2019 they are having makeup sex so expect a big powerful passionate explosion end of August. It is a good time for art, relationships, and a new talent.

February 18–29 Venus meets Saturn. This is a heavier aspect which causes all of us to reassess and reevaluate our relationships. If you are in a partnership this aspect can be challenging or maybe force you to take the relationship to the next level or break up. If you are not in a relationship, maybe you will meet someone older that can help you understand the deeper meaning of partnerships.

Mercury Retrograde –
The Trickster

Three times a year for about three weeks, Mercury, the planet of communication, appears to travel backwards. Of course, the planet does not really retrograde, but he appears to do so from the viewpoint of an earthling. Since Mercury is the planet that governs business, travel, connections, computers, communications, contracts, trade, and transactions, these aspects of our lives experience a great deal of hardships. It is not recommended that you sign any documents, get married or engaged, make big purchases, start important projects, enter a partnership in work, or publish during these periods.

People belonging to the signs that host Mercury while he is retrograding experience the effects of the retrograde motion more intensely. This year Mercury retrogrades in the water signs of Pisces, Cancer, and Scorpio. It is like dropping your cellphone in the toilet. As you can imagine, instruments of communication (Mercury) do not work well if they are in water. The miscommunications and glitches can generate a great deal of emotional confusion.

March 5 – 28: Mercury retrogrades in Pisces: miscommunications around your intuition, mystical experiences, addictions, enabling people's dependency and co-dependency. Lack of boundaries. On the other hand, it is not a bad time to start meditation or dancing. Any activity in water is recommended.

July 7 – 31: Mercury retrogrades in Leo (until July 19) and then moves to Cancer. Difficulties communicating with family members. You might find parenting is harder. Problems with land and real-estate. Shame, guilt, and passive aggressiveness.

October 31 – November 20: Mercury retrogrades in Scorpio. This is an intense retrograde as Scorpio's tarot card is "Death," and the retro starts right on Halloween and the Day of the Dead. Mercury in mythology is the *psychopompos*, he who delivers the soul across the river of death. You can expect some "visitations" from ancestors, angels, guides, and spirits in your dreams or meditations. However, some of the misunderstandings can be rather deadly…

If you must sign a lease, buy a car, or start a new job, it is still possible. I bought my car during Mercury Retro and it has been my best vehicle ever. But I did plant 88 trees on the day I signed the loan for the car (88 is the number of days it takes Mercury to orbit around the Sun), and I took extra care to look into every detail of the contract. You cannot be religious about astrology (or anything else for that matter), but you can heed her warnings. When it is raining take an umbrella. When in Mercury Retrograde, backup your computer and read the contract three times.

But it is not all darkness and gloom. During Mercury retrograde, it is a good time to edit, reevaluate, reexamine projects, relationships, and commitments. It is a good time to let go of people, substances, and habits you no longer need. It is a powerful time for manifestation, prayer, sending wishes and good intentions to family members and friends. While Mercury gives us a hard time with mundane communication, he supports inner or spiritual messages. If you believe in angels, they can hear you better during Mercury retrograde. If you believe in a higher self or in spiritual guides, then it is in retrograde that you can sacrifice your ego to get closer to your higher self. If you believe in life after death, now you can communicate with dead relatives, and if you know the way to DreamTime, Mercury Retrograde can be filled with lucid dreaming. Mercury retrograde is the best time for meditation and meeting with people or places you have known in past lifetimes.

Uranus, the Fool, going deeper into Taurus

Uranus is chaos and disorder. Uranus represents unpredictable and revolutionary behavior. Since 2010, Uranus has been in Aries, the sign of leaders and wars, and in May 2018, he moved into Taurus. While he was in Aries, we experienced the Arab Spring, the rise and (hopefully) fall of ISIS, mass immigration, as well as the attempts of Putin to become Stalin. We witnessed the rise of nationalism, the alternative right, alternative "truths," and a host of politicians that can be described as jokers and fools (the Tarot card of Uranus is the "Fool"). Since Taurus is the sign of finance, Uranus moving into the sign of the Bull can create a revolution in the world's economy, maybe giving a push to alternative financial systems.

From November 7, 2018 until March 6, 2019 Uranus retrograded back into Aries. That means that the first two months of 2019 are similar to whatever happened between 2010-2018. There could be aggressive, disruptive, warlike revolutions going on in your personal life and worldwide.

From March 6, 2019 until 2026, when Uranus is in Taurus, the sign of values, finance, art, design, and music, he provides the opportunity to shift and change these aspects of our lives. When the market is doing well, we call it the Bull Market as the bull or cow has always represented wealth, prosperity, and security. Uranus is here to shake the tree, but Taurus is a fixed earth sign, it is a sign that does not like to move or change. That is why we can expect a great deal of upheaval in the next few years as Uranus settles in this stubborn fixed earth sign.

Uranus in Taurus can also instigate big discoveries and breakthroughs in science, medicine (hair growth, Alzheimer's, Cancer, AIDS) and computing as well as the rise of an Artificial Intelligence-based economy. Of course, these trends can cause a great deal of upsets and revolutions and protests from people who will lose their jobs to robots. This process will continue even after April 2026, when Uranus moves to Gemini, the binary sign. During that decade (2026-2037), we can expect machines to process information faster than humans.

Right when Uranus moved into Taurus, the EU declared its GDPR (General Data Protection Regulations) that changed the way data can be mined and used by technology companies. California is said to follow soon. Two months later, the EU fined Google close to 5 billion dollars for violating antitrust rules. Donald Trump threatened trade war for many months, but only when Uranus moved into Taurus did he start the economic warfare.

The cycle of Uranus is 84 years. Last time Uranus was in Taurus was during the Great Depression and the onset of World War II. In the US, during Uranus in Taurus, the Social Security Act (1935) as well as the Banking Act became the law of the land, which changed the structure and power distribution in the Federal Reserve System. Another anecdote is that it was also the time the game Monopoly was created. History working along with Astrology can help us understand the present by looking at similar cycles in the past. For the last 9 decades the US dollar was the most dominant currency, but Uranus in the sign of finance and money will most likely change its status.

On a personal level, you need to rethink your finances and look into upgrading and innovating your talents. It is a time to expect some changes in your income and maybe take a leap of faith into a new field or a new source of revenue. Avoid any radical investments and be extra careful with cryptocurrency. Remember, Uranus is technology and Taurus is finance. We can expect more cyber (Uranus) attacks, especially on banks and financial institutions (Taurus). However, there could be more natural disasters and climate change as Taurus is said to be associated with Mother Nature.

Uranus in Taurus can give us the opportunity to revolutionize our artistic expression, our economy, and the treatment of our environment. While it is true that Uranus can be disruptive, his nature is to change things that don't work to our advantage. Uranus asks us to laugh at ourselves. If you can do it in the next 7 years, you should be fine. Just don't take things so personally.

2019 Affirmation:

I am open to signs, omens, and synchronicities that lead me to an authentic and meaningful life path. I welcome a career change that can improve my life as well as others. I am embracing opportunities to travel, learn, and teach. I am open to learning the lessons of compassion and being a vessel of unconditional love.

Now let's go...

In some of the sections I refer to the element of your sign. You will see that I would call an Aries, a fire sign, a Fire-Bender, or a Pisces, a water sign, a Water-Bender. This is a homage to the wonderful animated Nickelodeon TV series, (2005) *Avatar: The Last Air Bender*. If you have a kid or an active inner child, watch this wonderful series that helps balance the elements in an entertaining way. Aries, Leo, and Sagittarius are Fire-Benders; Gemini, Libra, and Aquarius are Air-Benders; Cancer, Scorpio, and Pisces are Water-Benders; Capricorn, Taurus, and Virgo are Earth-Benders.

2019 is a year when we can give birth to our inner child, creativity, and new opportunities in studies and teaching. 2019 is a year designed to help us connect to the goddess, to the *Shekinah*, the feminine aspect of the divine. This not only means we should be treating women with more respect and appreciation, but it also means connecting to your own feminine side regardless of gender. 2019 asks you to be receptive, artistic, and connect to the five senses. It will be great if you can add a new hobby to your life that can help you express your artistic and feminine side. It can be pottery, cooking, an instrument, painting, design, dance, yoga, swimming, gardening etc.

In Part II, the sections of the signs, you will read something like: Jupiter is in your house of career or Venus enters your house of health. In astrological charts, there are 12 houses that symbolize areas in our lives like career, health, relationships, etc. You don't have to worry about what it all means, but I added the name of the houses for you to have more clarity and maybe spark an interest in studying this ancient art.

part two

The Zodiac Signs

21TH MARCH – 19TH APRIL

ARIES

*Shine on You Crazy Diamond**

key phrase
I AM

element
Cardinal fire

planet
Mars

day
Tuesday

incentive
The spark

body parts
Head, blood, face, genitalia, muscles

color
Red

stone
Diamond

---

* Pink Floyd, 1975.

I AM MY MISSION.

2019 Integration:
Career and home

2019 continues your journey to reshape, rediscover, and manifest your career. Saturn, the Lord Karma, the grand teacher and the rectifier, is helping you rebuild the adobe of your professional life. You are the shepherd, the leader of the zodiac, and we expect you to boldly go where we dare not go. You are the pioneer and your job this year is to continue pushing the boundaries of what we know is possible. You are like a Knight of the Round Table, in search of the Holy Grail. Treading on a path already paved by another is an un-Aries thing to do, and this year you can truly push yourself to the limit in your career. If you are happy with your choices in your professional life, then this is the year to put a great deal of energy, planning, focus, and endurance toward making it happen. 2020 will continue your career journey, for this reason, I suggest you prepare for a marathon rather than a short sprint. If, however, you are not satisfied with your professional choices and want to make a change, this is a good year to make the jump. This is the year to find or continue your mission. In 2019, you can slay the dragon and save the prince/princess. Since Pluto (transformation) and Saturn (focus and hard lessons) and the eclipses (acceleration of processes) are all converging in your house of career, it is an auspicious time to make changes and fix your vocation as well as find a mission that can be your call to action.

Since Saturn is now transiting in the house of fathers, mentors, and authority figures, you might find some bosses or people who have power over you more difficult to handle. Try to use the eclipses in

January, July, and December to fix or heal relationships with father figures. It is hard to tell an Aries what to do and even more difficult for you to be bossed, but remember that you can help your bosses by carving out some independence or autonomy in your job, a place where you can have the freedom to lead and make decisions.

With so much focus on career, it is an interesting coincidence that you are also asked not to forget your family. With the North Node, the Head of the Dragon, moving into Cancer, ruler of your house of family, your home life is going to move into the foreground. It so happens that in astrology career is opposite to family. 2019's paradox for you is the need to focus on your home while not neglecting your career. There is no need to choose one or the other but rather integrate and balance the two. North Node shows us what our soul desires and not what our ego or bank account wants. 2019 is about the need to be needed. It is about feeling the warmth and security of a home. Home can be a small studio you rent as long as it feels like your fortress, your place of refuge, whatever wraps your soul. It is a good year to invest in real estate, especially if you plan to live there. 2019 is also good for renovation, moving in with someone, and of course, having a baby.

Uranus, the planet of unpredictability, left your sign in May 2018 after being there for 7 years. From March 6 2019, you can experience a stronger sense of stability and continuity. However, Uranus, due to a retrograde movement, has reentered your sign from November of 2018 and will be there until March 6 of 2019. That means that you will be revisited by a little bit of what you experienced with Uranus from 2010-2018. You might feel more chaos or unpredictable events in the first two months of 2019, but from March 6, things will settle down.

Jupiter brings you good news as he moved in late 2018 into Sagittarius, a member of your Fire Nation. This means that fortune and good luck can flow especially from studies, education, travel, multinational organizations, in-laws, justice, publishing, consulting, and teaching. Jupiter in Sagittarius can infuse you with a sense of optimism and opportunities. In December, Jupiter will move into your house of career. Yes! Career again. In December you might get some good news in your professional life.

Since Chiron is still in your sign, take extra care of your body and health. Be careful of head injuries, over training, or accidents. Those born between March 21 to 26 will experience Chiron stepping right on their sun. This aspect can also manifest as a strong connection to a shaman or a spiritual teacher. You may feel you are stepping into the role of a teacher, healer, or consultant. However, Chiron conjunct your sun can manifest as physical or emotional wounds.

 ## The 5 Eclipses – Your Emotional Landscape

Eclipses quicken processes and push events towards completion. They are wild-cards, amplifiers of whatever is happening in your life. They also weave stories through an endless magical tapestry of synchronicities and dreams. The eclipses this year are shifting into Cancer and Capricorn and since the North Node is in Cancer it asks us to focus on our feelings, security, compassion, and family. The Nodes represent the junction between the paths of the sun and the moon, the conjunction of the father and mother's influence. The North Node, also dubbed the Head of the Dragon, represents what our soul desires. The South Node, which is in the opposite side of the zodiac, hence in Capricorn, represents what our soul desires to let go. That means we must shed the dark side of Capricorn: fear, ignorance, lack of tolerance, fixation on the status quo, conservatism, and nationalism. Fear is partly designed to ensure our survival but being over preoccupied with ourselves and our survival can hamper the ability to see and relate to others. That is where Cancer comes in and teaches us compassion and empathy.

The eclipses this year in January, July, and December will bring us opportunities to face our fears, confront the devil, and come out winning using the magic of compassion, unconditional love, and loving-kindness.

The eclipses being in Cancer and Capricorn, fellow Cardinal signs, can make January, July, and December a bit more emotional and challenging as you also are a Cardinal sign. In other words, the eclipses create a square to your sun. This can cause you to be very reactive and impulsive. Please take heed around the eclipses this year. During the eclipses, you will feel an especially strong push and pull between home and career, feelings and responsibilities, mother and father, withdrawal and exposure. The eclipses can bring a great deal of fears and insecurities from early childhood.

January 5–6: Partial Solar Eclipse in Capricorn. This New Moon in Capricorn falls in your house of career and can present new opportunities to see a different aspect of your career which was hidden or eclipsed. A great time to try to improve your relationship with bosses and figures of authority.

January 20–21: Total Lunar Eclipse Leo/Cancer cusp. This full moon takes place right on the border between Cancer and Leo and falls between your house of children and love and the house of family. Lunar eclipses represent oppositions. In this case, it is pitting home and family opposite to career, mother versus father, your needs against those of your community's. This lunar eclipse can be especially emotional.

July 2, 2019: Total Solar Eclipse Cancer. This new moon marks a new beginning in your family life or emotional space as it falls in your house of home and family. The key phrase here is "I feel!" Good time to start a family and make a move to a new location.

July 16–17, 2019: Partial Lunar Eclipse Capricorn. This full moon in Capricorn again pits career versus home and family, mother figures versus father figures. You can see that this is a recurring theme of the year.

December 26, 2019: Annular Solar Eclipse Capricorn. This new moon in Capricorn falls in your house of career joining Saturn, Pluto, as well as Jupiter. A great deal of action and new beginnings even if it is the end of the year and holidays. The key phrase is "I Use." Try to use whatever resources you must to manifest new aspects in your career.

 ## Mercury Retrograde – Mental Landscape

During Mercury retrograde, it is not recommended to start new long-term projects, sign documents, make large purchases, get married, publish, start marketing campaigns, or release new products. Communications of all sorts are slower and filled with glitches and challenges. Computers crash; stock markets turn volatile: flights are delayed; traffic is worse than usual; accidents occur more often; and Murphy's Law takes hold of our lives. For example, the infamous Flash Crash of May 6, 2010 took place during Mercury retrograde in Taurus (the sign of money and the stock market). If you need to fly during Mercury retro, make sure you do your online check-in and take longer to reach the airport. Try to avoid overscheduling yourself or being overly critical and demanding. Also pay attention to your diet and food intake.

If you must start a new project, be as mindful as you can. Pay attention to small details and read in-between the lines if you must sign a document. Rewrite your emails; edit your texts; and think before you speak or post. In fact, it is better if you spend more time listening than talking. Life does not come to a halt during Mercury retrograde. You can still achieve a great deal. Mercury retro is like going on a vacation while it is raining. It is still possible but take an umbrella. However, it is a great time to edit, redo, reexamine yourself and your path, revisit old projects, and find lost objects. It is said that there are more coincidences and synchronicities while Mercury is retrograding. Try to focus on activities that have the prefix *re* – reevaluate, reedit, redo, reexamine, reconnect, regenerate, revisit, re-imagine, etc.

This year, Mercury is retrograding in water signs. Because you belong to the fire clan, it might be a bit more challenging as water and fire do not mix well. This combination can create steam which translates to overthinking. As a Fire-Bender, you might experience emotional moments during the retrogrades.

Between March 5 and March 28, Mercury retrogrades in Pisces, which falls in your house of past lives, letting go, and mysticism, creating miscommunications around your intuition, mystical experiences, and addictions. Be aware you might be enabling people's dependency and co-dependency. There may be a feeling of a lack of boundaries. Be careful of any relapses of past bad habits.

Between July 7 and July 31, Mercury retrogrades in Leo and then moves to Cancer, shifting the confusion from your house of love and children to the house of home and family. There could be more difficulties in communicating with family members. You might find parenting is harder. Problems with lands and real estate. Shame, guilt, and passive-aggressiveness can bring down your mood. Especially be careful around mid-July as the eclipses will combine their influence with that of Mercury retrograde, creating extra pressure and blowups.

Between October 31 and November 20, Mercury retrogrades in Scorpio in your house of sexuality, death, and investments. You can expect issues when dealing with inheritance, other people's money, investments, taxes, and insurance. There might be glitches with your intimacy and sexuality.

Unpredictability, Originality and a Touch of Chaos

In May 2018, Uranus moved into Taurus and will stay there until 2026, falling in your house of finance, talents, and self-worth. Please pay attention to your financial situation the next few years. Uranus is called "the Joker" or "the Fool." He is chaotic but also ingenious. You might suddenly get an "aha" moment that can help your finances and give you an original idea or a bright inkling about your earning potential. Even if you cannot manifest the idea right now, write it down. In the future, you might have time and resources to make it happen. However, due to Uranus' retrograde motion, he reentered your sign November 7, 2018 and will be in Aries until March 6, 2019. This means that, for the first two months of the year, Uranus will be creating a bit more chaos with your health, public image, and self-expression (you might be funny but also unpredictable). This aspect is especially strong for people born April 17–20.

From March 6, Uranus might inspire you to take a leap of faith into something totally new regarding your talents and finances, maybe a new field of study that can later translate into a new revenue stream. Uranus favors technology, innovation, and science. Maybe you can think of a great new application or an e-commerce business. It is also a good time to redo your website, give your Facebook page a face lift, and connect to social media.

Mars –
Energy and Passion

Mars, your ruler, governs vegetation, action, leadership, passion and aggression. Whenever he is transiting in your sign, you feel extra energy, enthusiasm, passion, and a strong sense of purpose. Sometimes it can feel as if you are high on caffeine or even something stronger. Mars can be pushy and make you say, do, or write impulsively, giving you extra confidence that can backfire.

This year, Mars, your planet, will be in your sign between January 1 and February 14. This aspect will allow you to push many projects forward and liberate you from oppressive situations. It is a great time to start a new exercise regime and assume a leadership role.

Below is a list of Mars' transits through the signs that can help you determine where to focus your energy. However, remember that even the best fighters need a general. Make sure you pace yourself and control your inner warrior.

  January 1 to Feb 14

This transit takes place in your house of body and personality. You might feel aggressive but also powerful enough to manifest your wishes. This is a good time to exercise or find a new physical activity that can improve your health. Be careful not to be at war with yourself.

  February 14 to March 31

This transit can give you a boost with your finances. It is a good time to invest in your talent and express your gifts as well as stand up for your values. Be careful of overspending. Since Uranus and Mars will be together in Taurus, be extra careful with accidents and mishaps.

 March 31 to May 16

This transit is a great time for winning arguments, helps with legal affairs, and can also provide you with extra energy in business and writing. However, your communication can ignite conflict. Be careful of fights with relatives, roommates, siblings, or neighbors.

  May 16 to July 1

Good time to renovate your home, office, or workspace. This Mars location can cause unnecessary conflict with your family. Mars will help you ride the dragon (North Node in Cancer) to reach a better place to live.

  July 1 to August 18

Romance! A wonderful time for recreational activities, sports, hobbies, and fun. You might feel a need to engage in risky endeavors so take heed of implosive behaviors. Love is in the air as well as creativity. Your inner child is active but be careful of injuries. You might experience conflict with lovers or your children.

  August 18 to October 4

This time can provide extra energy and passion in your work, as well as help you find a new way to serve. A great time for a new diet and changes of routine. Be careful of arguments and fights with employees and coworkers. Be extra careful of injuries, inflammations, and stress.

October 4 to November 19

A great time for projects with partners. Be careful of lawsuits or conflicts with your enemies. You might find yourself needing to spend
more time or energy with partners in work or in life. You partners
might initiate fights or, on the other hand, reignite your passion.

 November 19 to January 2, 2020

This is a powerful transit for Mars. Your passion, sexuality, and interest in intimacy is heightened. You will feel attractive and be able to
attract opportunities in finance, investments, and production. Your
own healing abilities can grow as well as the ability to help other
people tap into their talents and finance.

 # Venus: Money and Love

Venus is the ruler of pleasure, luxury, finance, talents, values, art,
and relationships. She is also associated with Maat, the goddess of
justice and law. Venus works in beauty cycles: the more you love
yourself, the more you believe in yourself. The better your self-image, the more you connect to your talents. The more you develop
and invest in your talents, the more money you can make. Venus'
message is: love yourself and money will follow.

This year, the goddess of beauty will be in your sign between April
20 to May 15, making you more attractive, helping you get a raise or
tap into a new talent. It is a great time for romance, making money,

and connecting to your artistic side. This is a good time for you to re-brand yourself, dress differently, change your hair, or get some new clothes. Not a bad time to indulge and pamper yourself (if it is healthy and does not harm you or anyone else).

Conclusion:

In 2019, you can give birth to a new stage in your career, especially if you can integrate travel, teaching, authenticity, and truth in your chosen profession. Be mindful of finances, especially in the second and third quarter of the year. 2019 also asks you to look into your family situation, your home, and how much you allow yourself to feel. A great time to relocate, especially in order to further and improve your career. Try to follow up on opportunities in education, teaching and traveling abroad.

20TH APRIL – 20TH MAY

TAURUS

Don't you know the joker laughs at you?*

key phrase
I HAVE

element
Fixed (unchangeable) earth

planet
Venus

day
Friday

incentive
Supporter

body parts
Throat, neck, thyroid gland

color
Red-orange

stone
Jade

---

* The Beatles, 1967.

54

I HAVE CHANGE.

2019 Integration: Authenticity in communication

2019 is a roller coaster for your tribe. Uranus, the planet of unpredictability and chaos, has moved in and out of your sign since May 2018 and will be hosted by you until 2026. However, from November 2018 until March 6, 2019, Uranus retrograded for a short visit back to Aries, giving you a bit of a break. From March 2019 onward, you are back under the influence of Uranus.

There is one way to describe Uranus in Taurus: ch-ch-ch changes. Uranus transiting in Taurus happens once in 84 years so unless you are in your late 80s you have not experienced this aspect before. Since Uranus also represents originality, futurism, and technology, the next few years offer a great opportunity to upgrade and update yourself and your life. This year people born April 20-26 will experience Uranus moving over their sun. This transit makes your life go through a roller coaster, sudden changes and twists. Be careful not to be a rebel without a cause.

Saturn, the Lord of Karma, the rectifier, continues his teaching in your house of truth and authenticity. These lessons started last year but are now becoming stronger as Jupiter, the planet of truth and philosophy, has moved into Sagittarius, the sign of authenticity. You are not only learning about truth. You are also supposed to be teaching this noble concept to others. This year revolves around education, connection to multinational organizations, exploring the world either by meeting foreigners and exposing yourself to different cultures or by traveling abroad. This year, you will have to ask yourself, what is important in my life? What am I willing to fight for? What is my moral compass? What are my mission statement and values? You will also have to confront liars, thieves, and people who are dishonest. They will be your devils, trying to tempt you from your path of self-discovery. Remember, when Saturn is in your house of truth, any lie, intentional or innocent, white, black, or gray can immediately cause a reaction. Bearing this in mind, be aware of cheating on lovers, taxes, friends, or yourself.

Since the eclipses are joining Saturn in Capricorn, there will be many opportunities this year to write and publish as well as connect to mass media, the internet, blogging, and more visibility over social media. Since Saturn is also in the house of in-laws, you will have to face some lessons through family members who do not share your DNA. Try to exercise compassion and patience. Believe me, you will be tested.

What is your 2019 paradox? Well, on one hand, Saturn is in your house of truth while, on the other hand, the North Node is in your house of communication. Lao Tzu once said: talking about the truth makes you a liar. You are trying to be honest and authentic, but you are also supposed to communicate, market, and promote, and we all know that these things demand some alternative truths if not straight-out lies. You will have to learn to be a truthful communicator and only sell things you would want to use yourself.

While Saturn teaches with the stick, Jupiter, the planet of fortune and luck, teaches with a carrot cake. This year, Jupiter is transiting in your house of sexuality and passion. This does not only mean you will have great sex but also that you might connect to your passion, to what motivates and drives you. Jupiter will help you develop your healing abilities as well as aid in shedding any negativity you carry from the past. Jupiter can also help your partners in life or in business increase their finances, thus indirectly improving your own income. 2019 is a great year for productions, investments, receiving an inheritance, and working with other people's talents and money.

The next 12 months give you the ability to die and, like a phoenix, resurrect out of the ashes.

In December, when Jupiter moves into Capricorn, you will be able to travel and connect to higher education.

 ## The 5 Eclipses – Your Emotional Landscape

Eclipses quicken processes and push events towards completion. They are wild-cards, amplifiers of whatever is happening in your life. They also weave stories through an endless magical tapestry of synchronicities and dreams. The eclipses this year are shifting into Cancer and Capricorn and since the North Node is in Cancer it asks us to focus on our feelings, security, compassion, and family. The Nodes represent the junction between the paths of the sun and the moon, the conjunction of the father and mother's influence. The North Node, also dubbed the Head of the Dragon, represents what our soul desires. The South Node, which is in the opposite side of the zodiac, hence in Capricorn, symbolizes what our soul desires to let go and quit. That means we must shed the dark side of Capricorn: fear, ignorance, lack of tolerance, fixation to the status quo, conservatism, and nationalism. Fear is partly designed to ensure our survival but being over preoccupied with ourselves and our survival can hamper the ability to see and relate to others. That is where Cancer comes in and teaches us compassion and empathy.

The eclipses this year in January, July, and December will bring us opportunities to face our fears, confront the devil, and come out winning using the magic of compassion, unconditional love, and loving-kindness.

During the eclipses, you will feel an especially strong push and pull between home and career, feelings and responsibilities, mother and father, withdrawal and exposure. The eclipses can bring a great deal of fears and insecurities from early childhood. Your eclipse opposition will also include the push and pull between sales, marketing, business, and truth.

January 5–6: Partial Solar Eclipse in Capricorn. This New Moon in Capricorn falls in your house of truth, education, and travel. If you plan to travel in January, please take extra care and be more mindful; however, the eclipse can unfold an opportunity to learn, teach, or connect to a new culture. Be aware there might be some issues with an in-law, especially male relatives.

January 20–21: Total Lunar Eclipse Leo/Cancer cusp. This full moon takes place right on the border between Cancer and Leo and falls between your houses of communication and family. Lunar eclipses represent oppositions. In this case it is pitting home and family versus career as well as your truth versus someone else's truth. Be careful not to be a zealot or preachy.

July 2, 2019: Total Solar Eclipse Cancer. This new moon marks a new beginning in your business, communication, writing, and contracts. The key phrase here is "I feel!" You must "feel" the business, writing project, or connections you engage in.

July 16–17, 2019: Partial Lunar Eclipse Capricorn. This full moon in Capricorn again pits career versus home and family, mother figures versus father figures, but it can also create tension between your "blood" relatives and in-laws. Make sure to avoid lies or people who want to steal your ideas, time, or energy.

December 26, 2019: Annular Solar Eclipse Capricorn. This new moon in Capricorn falls in your house of travel and philosophy. The key phrase is "I Use." Try to use your talents, connections, ideas, and resources to make a leap of faith in your career or education.

Maybe learn a new language or a new skill that can further your chosen path.

 ## Mercury Retrograde – Mental Landscape

During Mercury retrograde it is not recommended to start new long-term projects, sign documents, make large purchases, get married, publish, start marketing campaigns, or release new products. Communications of all sorts are slower and filled with glitches and challenges. Computers crash; stock markets turn volatile; flights are delayed; traffic is worse than usual; accidents occur more often; and Murphy's Law takes hold of our lives. For example, the infamous Flash Crash of May 6, 2010, took place during Mercury retrograde in your sign (Taurus is the sign of finance). If you need to fly during Mercury retro, make sure you do your online check-in and take longer to reach the airport. Try to avoid overscheduling yourself or being overly critical and demanding. Also pay attention to your diet and food intake.

If you must start a new project, be as mindful as you can. Pay attention to small details and read in-between the lines if you must sign a document. Rewrite your emails, edit your texts, and think before you speak. In fact, it is better if you spend more time listening than talking. Life does not come to a halt during Mercury retrograde. You can still achieve a great deal. Mercury retro is like going on a vacation while it is raining. It is still possible. Just make sure to take an umbrella. However, it is a great time to edit, redo, reexamine yourself and your path, revisit old projects, and find lost objects. It is said that there are more coincidences and more synchronicities when Mercury is retrograding. Try to focus on activities that have the prefix *re* – reevaluate, reedit, redo, reexamine, reconnect, regenerate, revisit, re-imagine, etc.

This year, Mercury is retrograding in water signs. Because you belong to the earth clan, this retrograde will feel a bit easier as water and earth, your element, mix well. As an Earth-Bender, you might experience some magical moments during the retrogrades, but be extra careful of the last retrograde in Scorpio as it is your opposite sign and will create a feeling of being pushed and pulled in different directions.

Between March 5 and March 28, Mercury retrogrades in Pisces, which falls in your house of friends, companies, governments, and organizations. Therefore, you can expect miscommunications and issues with these aspects I listed. Since this retrograde is in Pisces, the sign of mysticism, and transits in your house of manifestation of wishes, it is a good time for making dreams come true as long as you don't start any new projects.

Between July 7 and July 31, Mercury retrogrades in Leo and then moves to Cancer shifting the confusion from your house of home to the house of communication. This is a classic case of issues with contracts, miscommunication with siblings, roommates, and relatives. Be extra careful not to sign any documents. Be especially mindful around mid-July as the eclipses will combine their influence with that of Mercury retrograde creating extra pressure and blowups.

Between October 31 and November 20, Mercury retrogrades in Scorpio in your house of relationships and lawsuits. Be careful of unnecessary conflict with business and love partners. You might feel torn between two people, two projects, or in general a feeling that life is opposing you.

Unpredictability, Originality and a Touch of Chaos

Uranus, the planet of originality and unpredictability, has moved in May 2018 into your sign and will stay there until 2026. From November 7, 2018, until March 6, 2019, Uranus retrogrades back into Aries, which means that for the first few months of 2019, you have Uranus in your house of letting go. You might experience a sudden need to let go of things or cut some people out of your life. But from March, Uranus is back in your sign and in your first house of body and personality.

Uranus in the Tarot card is the "Fool." In playing cards, it is the "Joker." You will feel rebellious, a strong need to try new things, and you might feel like changing your look or public image, business card, and website. In addition, you may experience yourself as far more funny than usual. Since you are a fixed earth sign, sudden change is not always welcome, but you better get used to hosting the Joker in your sign for the next 7 years.

Since Uranus is the ruler of your house of career, one way of working with the changes Uranus presents is to implement them in your career or infuse your professional life with new forms of technologies and innovation. Be the change you want!

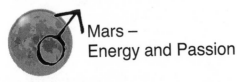

Mars – Energy and Passion

Mars governs vegetation, action, leadership, passion, and aggression. Whenever he is transiting in your sign, you feel extra energy, enthusiasm, passion, and a strong sense of purpose. It is as if you are high on caffeine or something stronger. Mars can be pushy and make you say, do, post, or write impulsively, giving you extra confidence that can backfire.

This year, Mars will be in your sign between February 14 and March 31. During this period, you will be able to push many projects forward and liberate yourself from oppressive situations. It is also a great time to start a new exercise regime and assume a leadership role.

Below is a list of Mars' transits through the signs that can help you determine where to focus your energy. However, remember that even the best fighters need a general. Make sure you pace yourself and control your inner warrior.

  January 1 to Feb 14

This is a call to action! This transit takes place in your house of letting go, past lifetimes, hidden enemies, hospitals, jails, and confinement. Be extra careful of injuries or accidents that can lead to a visit to the ER. You also must be aware that you might make hidden enemies. Memories from past lives might return as well as meetings with people you have known in past lives.

 February 14 to March 31

This transit takes place in your house of body and personality. You might feel aggressive but also powerful enough to manifest your wishes. This is a good time to exercise and find a new physical activity that can improve your health. Be careful not to be at war with yourself or too demanding of your body. However, having Mars in your sign can make you attractive and passionate. Since Uranus and Mars will be together in Taurus, be extra careful with accidents and mishaps.

March 31 to May 16

In general, Mars, the god of war in Gemini can help you win arguments, succeed in legal affairs, and have extra energy in business and writing. Be careful of fights with relatives, roommates, or neighbors. Mars in your second house can also give a boost to your finances. It is a time to invest in your talent and express your gifts as well as stand up for your values. Be careful not to overspend.

  May 16 to July 1

Good time to renovate your home, office or workspace. This Mars location can cause unnecessary conflict with your family. Since Mars is in your house of communication, he can help you get better contracts as well as improve your writing and business. Be careful of fights with relatives, roommates, or neighbors. Mars will help you ride the dragon (North Node in Cancer) and become a better messenger.

  July 1 to August 18

It is a good time for romance and sports, but since Mars is falling in your house of home and family, it is also a good time to renovate your home, office, or workspace. This Mars location can cause unnecessary conflict with your family, passive- aggressiveness, and make others feel guilty.

  August 18 to October 4

Extra energy and passion in your work, finding a new way to serve, pay attention to inflammations and stress-related health issues. However, since Mars is in your house of love, you can expect romance, recreational activities, sports, perhaps a new hobby, and lots of fun. Love is in the air as well as creativity.

 October 4 to November 19

A great time for projects with partners. Be careful of lawsuits or conflict with enemies. Since Mars is in transit in your house of work and service, you will experience extra energy and passion in your work, maybe even finding a new way to serve. It is a great time for diet and changes of routine. Be careful of arguments and fights with employees and coworkers. Be extra careful of injuries, inflammations, and blood-related diseases.

 November 19 to January 2, 2020

This is a powerful transit for Mars. Your passion, sexuality, and interest in intimacy is heightened. You will feel attractive and be able to attract opportunities in finance, investments, and production. Since this transit is in your house of relationships, you might have some confrontations with business or love partners. Mars in this house can cause difficulties with your antagonists and enemies. In addition, Mars is opposite to your sun; therefore, you might feel prone to outbursts of anger. Pace yourself!

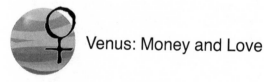 Venus: Money and Love

Venus is the ruler of pleasure, luxury, finance, talents, values, art, and relationships. She is also the ruler of your sign and you can see yourself as the child of the goddess of love. Venus works in beauty cycles: the more you love yourself, the more you believe in yourself.

The better your self-image, the more you connect to your talents. The more you develop and invest in your talents, the more money you can make. Venus' message is: love yourself and money will follow.

This year, the goddess of beauty will be in your sign between May 15 and June 9, making you more attractive, helping you get a raise or tap into a new talent. It is a great time for romance, making money, and connecting to your artistic side. This is a good time for you to rebrand yourself, dress differently, change your hair, and get some new clothes. Not a bad time to indulge and pamper yourself (if it is healthy and does not harm you or anyone else).

Conclusion:

If you ever wanted to move to a different country or explore higher education, this is a very good year to do that. 2019 is the year that can help you redefine your philosophy, as well as become a more authentic individual. 2019 can make you a teacher, consultant, a sage, and an adviser. In addition, your passion, sexuality, and magical abilities will grow this year. There is even a possibility for a bequest that can manifest as an inheritance, a gift from past lifetime, or an ability to benefit from a joint artistic or financial project.

21ᵀᴴ MAY – 20ᵀᴴ JUNE

GEMINI ♊

Let it be, let it be, speaking words of wisdom, let it be*

Key phrase
I THINK

Element
Mutable (changeable) air

Planet
Mercury, the messenger of gods

Day
Wednesday

Incentive
Flexibility

Body parts
Arms, lungs, nervous system

Color
Orange

Stone
Rock crystal

---

* The Beatles, 1970.

I THINK OF THINKING LESS.

 2019 Integration:
My talents and my
partner's talents

Dearest Geminis, you will find 2019 very curious and interesting. This is great news for you, as a mutable sign, who else on the zodiac appreciates change and movement like you? Saturn, the Lord of karma, the rectifier according to Kabbalah, is deep in your house of death and transformation. Sounds spooky, and indeed it is, considering that the eclipses are going to join Saturn in your house of the underworld, which has already been hosting Pluto, the Lord of death, since 2008. Some say that Gemini, an air sign, is the most superficial sign, an archetype that is interested in knowing just enough about every subject under the sun so they can swing a meaningful conversation with anyone they meet. I will not say if I feel this is true or false, but I can promise you one thing. Once in 30 years, you get deeper than any sign (even Scorpio). Now is the time to take a deep breath and dive deep. Saturn in the house of sexuality, death, transformation, intimacy, and the occult, is not your natural place to hang out. But this year you will experience a great deal of interest in investigation, hermetic studies, healing and therapy, death and the afterlife, as well as all forms of transformation. This year you are shedding and next year you will resurrect.

Saturn in your house of transformation can help you dive deeper into a new research field. Saturn can focus your energy in investments, production, and working with other people's money and talents. But Saturn can teach you some harsh lessons with taxes, insurance, as well as grief. So be extra careful.

Saturn will also want you to examine your passion and sexuality. For some Geminis it will feel like being in a cocoon, asexual and divorced from their passion. For other Geminis (yes, you are a double sign) this same aspect can transform how you view your sexuality, what attracts you, and maybe even get you to experience passion in a fresh way.

Adding to the karmic position of Saturn in your house of death is the transit of Uranus, the joker and lord of chaos into your house of mysticism and past lifetimes. There is a lot of letting go happening this year so if you want to purge, purify, detox, and cut from obstacles that keep you stagnant, 2019 is the year you have been waiting for.

The paradox for you this year is around finance, talent, and self-worth. Paradoxes are easy for you to handle, so I am sure you will not only be fine but also enjoy this inconsistency. On one hand, you have Saturn, Pluto, most of the eclipses, and from December, Jupiter activating and focusing you on the house of death, sexuality, as well as other people's money and talents. There is no doubt a great deal of attention that will be directed in these aspects of your life. But on the other hand, you have the South Node in that same house, which asks you to let go of your interest in other people's money and talents, to let go of your sexuality, and to focus on your own talents and self-worth. You are asked to let go of your PARTNER's finance and talents and instead focus on YOUR money, talents, and self-worth. 2019 is about integrating your needs with your partner's needs, whether the partner is in life or in business.

Jupiter, the planet of expansion and opportunities, is now transiting in your house of relationships and partnerships. This is great news if you were wanting to find a life partner or a partner in work. If you have a partner, it might get serious this year. In addition, Jupiter can help with lawsuits or as protection against enemies or people who block you. But because Jupiter is in your opposite sign, you must be careful not to be over-the-top and overconfident. You might feel an inflated sense of importance that can also lead to over-optimism and overcommitting to too many projects. In December, when Jupiter moves into Capricorn, he will join Saturn in the house of death and allow you to go into the final stage of your rite of passage.

Since Mercury is the ruler of your sign, all Mercury retrogrades are pivotal times for you. The list is provided below, but since the retrogrades are all taking place under water signs, this year is colored by wet communications. What I mean is that in 2019 your communication should be as emotional as possible, especially since the North Node moved into Cancer, the sign whose key phrase is "I feel."

The 5 Eclipses –
Your Emotional Landscape

Eclipses quicken processes and push events towards completion. They are wild-cards, amplifiers of whatever is happening in your life. They also weave stories through an endless magical tapestry of synchronicities and dreams. The eclipses this year are shifting into Cancer and Capricorn and since the North Node is in Cancer it asks us to focus on our feelings, security, compassion, and family. The Nodes represent the junction between the paths of the sun and the moon, the conjunction of the father and mother's influence. The North Node, also dubbed the Head of the Dragon, represents what our soul desires. The South Node, which is in the opposite side of the zodiac, hence in Capricorn, represents what our soul desires to let go. That means we must shed the dark side of Capricorn: fear, ignorance, lack of tolerance, fixation to the status quo, conservatism, and nationalism. Fear is partly designed to ensure our survival but being over preoccupied with ourselves and our survival can hamper the ability to see and relate to others. That is where Cancer comes in and teaches us compassion and empathy.

The eclipses this year in January, July, and December will bring us opportunities to face our fears, confront the devil, and come out winning using the magic of compassion, unconditional love and loving-kindness.

During the eclipses, you will feel an especially strong push and pull between home and career, feelings and responsibilities, mother and father, withdrawal and exposure. The eclipses can bring a great deal of fears and insecurities from early childhood.

January 5–6: Partial Solar Eclipse in Capricorn. This New Moon in Capricorn falls in your house of sexuality, passion, death, and transformation. We already saw that Saturn and Pluto are also in your house of transformation. The eclipses are going to be pointers or landmarks in the process of cutting off what is not helping you grow. Death, intimacy, investments, and shedding are in the spotlight around the eclipse. It is a good time to start a joint financial or artistic project.

January 20–21: Total Lunar Eclipse Leo/Cancer cusp. This full moon takes place right on the border between Cancer and Leo and falls between your houses of money and communication. Lunar eclipses represent oppositions. In this case, it is pitting home and family opposite to career, mother versus father, your needs and your community's needs. But since there is an emphasis on the houses of finance and communication, you might have to deal with oppositions between your finance and your partner's money. Lies, miscommunications in business, and sudden revelations about contracts.

July 2, 2019 — Total Solar Eclipse Cancer. This new moon marks a new beginning with your finances, income, talent, or self-worth. Your ego might be a bit more sensitive during the eclipse. The key phrase here is "I feel!" If you can feel a talent or an opportunity with finance, it can actually be a good boost.

July 16–17, 2019 — Partial Lunar Eclipse Capricorn. This full moon in Capricorn again pits career versus home and family, mother figures versus father figures. But since it is falling in the axis of finance, it can create some issues around investments or joint financial/artistic affairs. There will be some death and letting go.

December 26, 2019 — Annular Solar Eclipse Capricorn. This new moon in Capricorn falls in your house of death and transformation. It can be magical as the eclipse new moon is joining Saturn, Pluto, as well as Jupiter in the house of sexuality and death. A great deal of action and new beginning even if it is the end of the year and holidays. The key phrase is "I Use." Try to use whatever resources you have to manifest new aspects with investments and production. Maybe your passion will ignite and reveal some magical abilities.

 ## Mercury Retrograde – Mental Landscape

Let's talk a bit about Mercury, your planet, the messenger of the gods and goddesses. During Mercury retrograde it is not recommended to start new long-term projects, sign documents, make large purchases, get married, publish, start marketing campaigns, or release new products. Computers crash; stock markets turn volatile; flights are delayed; traffic is worse than usual; accidents occur more often; and Murphy's Law takes hold of our lives. For example, the infamous Flash Crash of May 6, 2010, took place during Mercury retrograde in Taurus (the sign of money and the stock market). If you need to fly during Mercury retro, and Geminis always do, take a longer time to reach the airport. Try to avoid overscheduling yourself or being overly critical and demanding. Also pay attention to your diet and food intake.

If you must start a new project, be as mindful as you can. Pay attention to small details and read in-between the lines if you must sign a document. Rewrite your emails, edit your texts, and think before you speak. In fact, it is better if you spend more time listening than talking. Life does not come to a halt during Mercury retrograde. You can still achieve a great deal. Mercury retro is like going on a vacation while it is raining. It is still possible but not much fun. However, it is a great time to edit, redo, reexamine yourself and your path, revisit old projects, and find lost objects. It is said that there are more coincidences and synchronicities while Mercury is retrograding. Try to focus on activities that have the prefix re – reevaluate, reedit, redo, reexamine, reconnect, regenerate, revisit, re-imagine, etc.

This year, Mercury is retrograding in water signs. Because you belong to the air clan, it might be a bit more challenging as water and air do not mix well. This combination can create bubbles and illusions and they tend to burst during Mercury retro.

Between March 5 and March 28, Mercury retrogrades in Pisces, which falls in your house of career. There might be miscommunication, cancelled projects, and difficulties with your career. Also, pay attention to misunderstandings with bosses or father figures.

Between July 7 and July 31, Mercury retrogrades in Leo and then moves to Cancer shifting the confusion from your house of communication to the house of finance. This is a pretty powerful retro and can cause more emotional stress. Be extra careful with finances and expenses. Be especially careful around mid-July as the eclipses will combine their influence with that of Mercury retrograde, creating extra pressure and blowups.

Between October 31 and November 20, Mercury retrogrades in Scorpio in your house of work, health, diet, and employees. Be extra attentive to manipulation and secrets in your workspace or with people who serve you. Mind your digestive system as well as intestines. Be vigilant with your diet and health.

Unpredictability, Originality and a Touch of Chaos

In May 2018, Uranus moved into Taurus and will stay there until 2026, falling in your house of letting go, mysticism, past lifetimes, jails, and confinement. Uranus will stay there for almost 7 years. So you better get used to it. Uranus is called "the Joker" or "the Fool." He is chaotic but also ingenious. The placement of Uranus in your house of letting go can cause you to become a spiritual gangster or renegade. You might feel like you want to rebel against fate or your destiny. You might suddenly get "aha" moments or epiphanies regarding your life. You will feel more intuitive but will find it hard to act according to these insights.

Due to Uranus' retrograde motion, he reentered your house of community and people between November 7, 2018 and will be there until March 6, 2019. This means that, for the first two months of the year, there will be more chaos and craziness with friends, governments, or corporations. You might meet new, interesting, and ingenious people, but there could be unpredictability with some communities or groups around you. After March 6, Uranus returns to the house of letting go and will be there until April 2026.

 Mars –
Energy and Passion

Mars governs vegetation, action, leadership, passion, and aggression. Whenever he is transiting in your sign, you feel extra energy, enthusiasm, passion, and a strong sense of purpose. Sometimes it can feel as if you are high on caffeine or even something stronger. Mars can be pushy and make you say, do, or write impulsively, giving you extra confidence that can backfire.

This year will be in your sign between March 31 and May 16. This aspect will allow you to push many projects forward and liberate you from oppressive situations. It is a great time to start a new exercise regime and assume a leadership role.

Below is a list of Mars' transits through the signs that can help you determine where to focus your energy throughout 2019. However, remember that even the best fighters need a general. Make sure you pace yourself and control your inner warrior.

 January 1 to Feb 14

You might feel aggressive but also powerful enough to manifest your wishes. This is a good time to exercise or find a new physical activity that can improve your health. Since Mars falls in your house of friends and communities, you might experience conflict and strife with friends or in groups to which you belong. It is a good time for nonprofit work and altruism.

 February 14 to March 31

This transit can help you boost your finances. It is a good time to invest in your talent and express your gifts as well as stand up for your values. Be careful of overspending. Mars is now in your house of mysticism and letting go. You might recognize people you have known in past lives. It is a good time for meditation, listening to your intuition, and actively letting go of things that hold you back. Since Uranus and Mars will be together in Taurus, be extra careful with accidents and mishaps.

  March 31 to May 16

Mars in your sign is a great time for winning arguments, getting help with legal affairs, and can also provide you with extra energy in business and writing. Be careful of fights with relatives, roommates, siblings, or neighbors. Since Mars is now transiting in your first house, be extra careful with your body, injuries, over-training, or being at war with yourself. You might come across as too aggressive.

  May 16 to July 1

Good time to renovate your home, office, or workspace. This Mars location can cause unnecessary conflict with your family. Mars is transiting in your house of finance. Be careful not to overspend, but you might have energy to start new projects that can generate income. Mars will help you ride the dragon (North Node in Cancer) and fly towards a new financial opportunity.

  July 1 to August 18

A wonderful time for recreational activities, sports, hobbies and fun. You might feel a need to engage in risky endeavors so take heed of implosive behaviors. Since Mars is now in your house of communication, you might come across as verbally abusive. Anger management is important in the next few weeks. Be careful of issues in contracts or fights with siblings or relatives.

August 18 to October 4

Mars can give you extra energy and passion in your work as well as help you find a new way to serve. A great time for diet and changes of routine. Be careful of arguments and fights with employees and coworkers. Since Mars is in your house of home and family, be careful of arguments with family members. However, it is a good time for a move.

 October 4 to November 19

A great time for projects with partners. Be careful of lawsuits or conflict with enemies. You might find yourself needing to spend more time or energy with partners in work or in life. Since Mars is now in your house of love, it can generate powerful romantic feelings. It is a good time for sports, fun, and recreation. A good time for risky projects but don't act out of impatience.

 November 19 to January 2, 2020

This is a powerful transit for Mars. Your passion, sexuality, and interest in intimacy is heightened. You will feel attractive and be able to attract opportunities in finance, investments, and production. Since Mars is in your house of work and health, he can bring about new energy with work projects. Take heed not to create war with employees or people who serve you.

Venus: Money and Love

Venus is the ruler of pleasure, luxury, finance, talents, values, art, and relationships. She is also associated with Maat, the goddess of justice and law. Venus works in beauty cycles: the more you love yourself, the more you believe in yourself. The better your self-image, the more you connect to your talents. The more you develop and invest in your talents, the more money you can make. Venus' message is: love yourself and money will follow.

This year, the goddess of beauty will be in your sign between June 9 to July 3, making you more attractive, helping you get a raise or tap into a new talent. It is a great time for romance, making money, and connecting to your artistic side. This is a good time for you to re-brand yourself, dress differently, change your hair, and get some new clothes. Not a bad time to indulge and pamper yourself (if it is healthy and does not harm you or anyone else).

Conclusion:

This is a powerful year for you, messengers of the gods. With Saturn in your house of death, sexuality, and magic and Uranus in your house of past lives, you are really feeling the *Twilight Zone* vibe this year. It is a year where you will have to deal with depth, intimacy, transformation, and relationships. You will not find life black and white, 0 or 1, true or false, but rather more complicated and interesting. This year can bring you a wonderful boost in your relationships as well as a new understanding about your finances and talents.

21TH JUNE – 22ND JULY

CANCER

*Love, love me do, you know I love you**

key phrase
I FEEL

element
Cardinal water

planet
The Moon, which gives us light in the darkest hour

day
Monday

incentive
Birth

body parts
Ribs, stomach, chest, internal organs, womb

color
Orange-yellow

stone
Pearl

* The Beatles, 1962.

78

2019 Integration:
I and thou

2019 is an eventful year for you guys. I know you like to take your time in almost everything you are doing, but this year with the eclipses in your sign, things are moving faster than before. This year, there is a lot of action in Capricorn, your opposite sign. With Saturn, Pluto, some of the eclipses, and in December, Jupiter, all converging in Capricorn, the energies overflow into your sign. In addition, the North Node, also dubbed Head of the Dragon, is transiting into your sign for the first time since 2000-2001. It is vital that you go back 19, 38, and 57 years to see what the dragon wanted to teach you. The Head of the Dragon lunar node, as we saw earlier, is a mathematical point in the chart that tells us what our soul desires to learn. Since November 2018, as the Dragon moved into Cancer and now breathes water, we all must learn the lessons taught by your sign. That means that for the next two years we look up to you, Cancer, to tell us how to behave. It means that you are now the mother/father of dragons. It is up to you to tame, fly, navigate, feed, and control the dragon. You need to set an example with your compassion, unconditional love, acceptance, parenting skills, healing talents, nourishing abilities, and forgiveness. And believe me, we will test you again and again to see if you still love us, even though we are putting you through hell.

Saturn, the Lord Karma, the rectifier according to Kabbalah, is continuing his track through your house of relationships and partnership. It is the seventh house that the famous song from the musical *Hair*, "Aquarius," is mentioning. This is your time to look deep into all your significant relationships in work and in life, especially contractual relationships, and scrutinize them. Many of you will get married, many will get a divorce, some will do both in the next two years. Saturn is trying to rectify how you deal with your partners, those you chose to mirror your true self back to you. This is a year when you can break patterns in relationships and drastically improve your connections to significant others, especially during the eclipses in January, July, and December. The transit of Saturn in this house can also manifest as challenges from your enemies, legal issues, and lawsuits. Take heed and get a good lawyer.

Your paradox this year is due to the North Node moving into your sign. On the one hand, you are asked by all the planets in Capricorn in your house of relationship to focus on partnership and significant others. On the other hand, the North Node in your sign asks you to focus on you and what you need and let go of relationships and partnership. What will it be? "I" or "thou." This will be a hard balance for you since you need to be needed and you love to give. However, can you also give without being drained? Can you give to yourself as well? Like a mother who needs to know when to wean her baby, you will have to learn to say "enough."

Jupiter, the planet of gifts and opportunities, is moving into your house of health and work. This can help you heal, fix your diet, as well as shine in your work. It is a good year to hire help or an assistant. It also gives you a boost to change and improve your working conditions and perhaps get a promotion.

In December 2019, when Jupiter enters Capricorn he will ingress into your house of relationships. This will help you win any pending lawsuits or challenges from antagonists and create new opportunities with relationships and love partners.

The 5 Eclipses –
Your Emotional Landscape

Since you are ruled by the moon, solar and lunar eclipses are always very sensitive times for you. Eclipses quicken processes and push events towards completion. They are wild-cards, amplifiers of whatever is happening in your life. They also weave stories through an endless magical tapestry of synchronicities and dreams. The eclipses this year are shifting into your sign and your opposite sign, Capricorn. The North Node represents the junction between the paths of the sun and the moon, the conjunction of the father and mother's influence. The North Node, as was mentioned, represents what our soul desires, while the South Node in Capricorn represents what our soul desires to let go. That means this year we must shed the dark side of Capricorn: fear, ignorance, lack of tolerance, fixation to the status quo, conservatism, and nationalism. Fear is partly designed to ensure our survival but being over preoccupied with yourself and your survival can hamper your ability to see and relate to others. That is where your tribe, Cancer, comes in and teaches us compassion and empathy, he ability to walk in other people's shoes. The eclipses this year in January, July, and December will bring us opportunities to face our fears, confront the devil, and come out winning using the magic of compassion and unconditional love.

This year is super crucial for your emotional development. This year your EQ (emotional intelligence) will rise dramatically. You are already very psychic and intuitive and this year you will feel how your gut feelings will be your best guide. Listen to your intuition!

During the eclipses, you will feel an especially strong push and pull between home and career, feelings and responsibilities, mother and father, withdrawal versus exposure. The eclipses can bring a great deal of fears and insecurities from early childhood. Your paradox of "I" versus "thou" will be especially strong during the eclipses.

January 5–6: Partial Solar Eclipse in Capricorn. This New Moon in Capricorn falls in your house of relationships and partnerships as well as enemies. A new partner might come into your life or a new phase in your significant relationships.

January 20–21: Total Lunar Eclipse Leo/Cancer cusp. This full moon takes place right on the border between your sign and Leo and falls between your houses of finance and body. The lunar eclipses represent oppositions. In this case, it is pitting home and family opposite to career, mother versus father, your needs and your community's needs. This lunar eclipse can be especially emotional. Again, relationships can be in the spotlight as well as your needs versus your partner needs and your finances opposite to your partner's income.

July 2, 2019: Total Solar Eclipse Cancer. This new moon marks a new beginning in your family life or emotional space as it falls in your house of family. This is the most important new moon of the year and maybe in the last 19 years. It represents an opportunity to rebrand yourself, a new way of presenting yourself and your public image.

July 16–17, 2019: Partial Lunar Eclipse Capricorn. This full moon in Capricorn again pits career versus home and family, mother figures versus father figures. You can see that this is a recurring theme of the year. This time, the sun is in your sign and the moon is in Capricorn. It can bring some fears and egocentric behavior on your part. Remember the lessons of compassion and acceptance.

December 26, 2019: Annular Solar Eclipse Capricorn. This new moon in Capricorn falls in your house of relationships and marriage. It can bring a new partner in life or business or a new beginning for your existing partner.

Mercury Retrograde – Mental Landscape

During Mercury retrograde, it is not recommended to start new long-term projects, sign documents, make large purchases, get married, publish, start marketing campaigns, or release new products. Computers crash; stock markets turn volatile; flights are delayed; traffic is worse than usual; accidents occur more often; and Murphy's Law takes hold of our lives. For example, the infamous Flash Crash of May 6, 2010, took place during Mercury retrograde in Taurus (the sign of money and the stock market). If you need to fly during Mercury retro, make sure you do your online check-in and take longer to reach the airport. Try to avoid overscheduling yourself or being over-critical and demanding. Also pay attention to your diet and food intake.

If you must start a new project, be as mindful as you can. Pay attention to small details and read in-between the lines if you must sign a document. Rewrite your emails, edit your texts, and think before you speak. In fact, it is better if you spend more time listening than talking. Life does not come to a halt during Mercury retrograde. You can still achieve a great deal. Mercury retro is like going on a vacation while it is raining. It is still possible but not much fun. However, it is a great time to edit, redo, reexamine yourself and your path, revisit old projects, and find lost objects. It is said that there are more coincidences and synchronicities while Mercury is retrograding. Try to focus on activities that have the prefix *re* – reevaluate, reedit, redo, reexamine, reconnect, regenerate, revisit, re-imagine, etc.

This year, Mercury is retrograding in water signs, and since you are a Water-Bender, you might be able to flow through the retrograde with relative ease. However, the second Mercury Retrograde falls in your sign while the eclipses are taking place, so please watch mid-July as it might feel super chaotic.

Between March 5 and March 28, Mercury retrogrades in Pisces, which falls in your house of travel, education, philosophy, and in-laws. If you plan to travel or have any tests, take extra time to prepare and coordinate. There might be misunderstandings with multinational corporations, foreigners, mentors, teachers, and in-laws.

Between July 7 and July 31, Mercury retrogrades in Leo and then moves to Cancer shifting the confusion from your house of money, talents, and self-worth into the house of your body and personality. You might feel confused about your path in life. People will misunderstand you, but be extra careful not to buy expensive things. Be especially careful around mid-July as the eclipses will combine their influence with that of Mercury retrograde creating extra pressure and blowups.

Between October 31 and November 20, Mercury retrogrades in Scorpio in your house of work and health. Take extra care with your diet and routine. There may be some misunderstandings with co-workers or employees.

 Unpredictability, Originality and a Touch of Chaos

In May 2018, Uranus moved into Taurus and will stay there until 2026, falling in your house of friends, community, wishes, and hope. This means that there is unpredictability around these aspects. Friends zooming in and out of your life. If you work in a large organization or corporation, there might be sudden changes. By the same token, there could also be unpredictable and unexpected wishes that come true.

Uranus is called "the Joker" or "the Fool." It is chaotic but also ingenious. You might suddenly get "aha" moments that can help your standing in your community or organization. You will notice that funnier and more colorful people are attracted to your company. But since Uranus is also the rebel, you might feel an urge to rebel against governments, organizations, or a corporation. Be careful not to be a rebel without a cause. You also might find a cause or a project for the empowerment of people or something you want to fight for to improve humanity.

Due to Uranus' retrograde motion, he reentered your house of career in November 7, 2018 and will be there until March 6, 2019. This means that for the first two months of the year, Uranus will be creating a bit more chaos in your professional life with unpredictable situations in your vocation. This aspect can also mean a need to rebel against a boss or a father figure.

Uranus favors technology, innovation, and science. Maybe you can think of a great new application or an e-commerce business or introducing something new into your career.

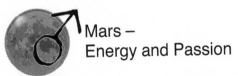

Mars –
Energy and Passion

Mars governs vegetation, action, leadership, passion, and aggression. Whenever he is transiting in your sign, you feel extra energy, enthusiasm, and passion with a strong sense of purpose. Sometimes it can feel as if you are high on caffeine or even something stronger. Mars can be pushy and make you say, do, or write impulsively. Mars can also give you extra confidence that can backfire.

This year Mars will be in your sign between May 16 and July 1. This aspect will allow you to push many projects forward and liberate you from oppressive situations. It is a great time to start a new exercise regime and assume a leadership role.

Below is a list of Mars' transits through the signs that can help you determine where to focus your energy. However, remember that even the best fighters need a general. Make sure you pace yourself and control your inner warrior.

  January 1 to Feb 14

You might feel aggressive but also powerful enough to manifest your wishes. This is a good time to exercise or find a new physical activity that can improve your health. Mars is in your house of career and can help you feel like a bundle of energy. Be careful of conflict with authority figures.

  February 14 to March 31

This transit can help you boost your finances. It is a good time to invest in your talent and express your gifts as well as stand up for your values. Mars is placed in your house of friends and organizations. Mars can help you get a promotion or a new leadership position but can also cause strife with friends or colleagues. Since Uranus and Mars will be together in Taurus, be extra careful with accidents and mishaps.

  March 31 to May 16

It is a great time for winning arguments, getting help with legal affairs, and can also provide you with extra energy in business and writing. Mars is in your house of letting go and mystical experiences. It is a good time for meditation and retreats of all kind.

 May 16 to July 1

Good time to renovate your home, office or workspace. This Mars location can cause unnecessary conflict with your family. Mars is now in your first house, which can make you feel connected to leadership abilities. You may come across as extra aggressive but also very passionate. Mars will help you ride the dragon (North Node in Cancer) and help you get the energy and strength to assert yourself.

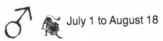 July 1 to August 18

A wonderful time for recreational activities, sports, hobbies and fun. You might feel a need to engage in risky endeavors so take heed of implosive behaviors. Mars is now in your house of finance, try to avoid spending money impulsively. However, Mars can help you shine and be noticed for your talents.

 August 18 to October 4

This time can provide extra energy and passion in your work, as well as help you find a new way to serve. A great time for diet and changes of routine. Be careful of arguments and fights with employees and coworkers. Mars is transiting in your house of communication and writing. Mars can bring new energy around sales and marketing. Be careful of fights with siblings, roommates, or relatives.

 October 4 to November 19

A great time for projects with partners. Be careful of lawsuits or conflict with enemies. You might find yourself needing to spend more time or energy with partners in work or in life. Mars is traveling in your house of home and family, giving you energy to make a move, renovate your living space, or deal with real estate.

  November 19 to January 2, 2020

This is a powerful transit for Mars. Your passion, sexuality, and interest in intimacy is heightened. Mars is in your house of love and romance and he can make you irresistible! This is also the house of sports; therefore, it is a good time for movement or starting a new activity.

 ## Venus: Money and Love

Venus is the ruler of pleasure, luxury, finance, talents, values, art, and relationships. She is also associated with Maat, the goddess of justice and law. Venus works in beauty cycles: the more you love yourself, the more you believe in yourself. The better your self-image, the more you connect to your talents. The more you develop and invest in your talents, the more money you can make. Venus' message is: love yourself and money will follow.

This year, the goddess of beauty will be in your sign between July 3 and July 28, making you more attractive, helping you get a raise or tap into a new talent. It is a great time for romance, making money, and connecting to your artistic side. This is a good time for you to re-brand yourself, dress differently, change your hair, or get some new clothes. Not a bad time to indulge and pamper yourself (if it is healthy and does not harm you or anyone else).

Conclusion:

2019 is the year that you both learn and teach others the qualities of your sign: compassion and unconditional love. It is a year that forces you to look deep into all your close associations from business partners to marriage and love. There could be some major positive changes with work, maybe even a promotion. 2019 is also a good year for healing physically and mentally.

23RD JULY – 22ND AUGUST

LEO

*Carried away by a moonlight shadow**

key phrase
I WILL

element
Fixed (unchangeable) fire

planet
The Sun

day
Sunday

incentive
Dynasty

body parts
Heart and spine

color
Golden and yellow

stone
Tiger eye

---
* Mike Oldfield, 1983.

I WILL SERVE!

 ## 2019 Integration: Retreating and engaging

The last two years were a roller coaster for the zodiacal felines. In 2017 and 2018, the North Node was in your sign for the first time since 1998 and it was shifting the eclipses to point at you. In the last two years, especially in February and July/August, you felt life accelerate, pushing you to new frontiers. Now that the North Node has moved away from you and into Cancer, you will feel less stress and extra responsibilities. In 2019 you can lick your wounds and rest.

Saturn, the Lord of Karma, the rectifier according to Kabbalah, is helping you fix your work, diet, health, and routine. Saturn is not a good or a bad planet. He teaches us what needs to be assimilated in order to grow. Saturn helps us identify and break patterns. In 2018, this year as well as in 2020, you are asked to change things in the way you work, in your routine, and in your schedule. The key word for the next year continues to be "Service." I know that you are of royal blood and that you should be served, but once in 30 years you learn what service is and how it works. In 2019 you must master this concept. Your health is determined by how you *serve* your body: what you eat and how you exercise. Your work and success in your job is conditioned by how you *serve* your mission or how you let your employees *serve* you. There might be a change in where and what you do for work. There could also be some challenges with your employees or a need to change people who work for you or under you. There could also be a possibility that people under you in work or your coworkers have a hard time in their personal lives that could affect their ability to work.

Since Saturn is in your house of health, he can bring some difficulties in that sphere. So please take extra time for healing, working out, eating well, or rejuvenating. And here your paradox manifests for 2019. On one hand, the cluster of planets in your house of work and health focuses you on engaging with service and being always available for others. On the other hand, the lunar nodes ask you to let go of work and service and retreat, connect to the mystic in you, focus on spirituality, and go meditate under a tree for a year or two.

Having Uranus, the joker, in your house of career while Saturn is in your house of work can be a bit strange in your professional life. It can manifest as a chaotic boss or sudden changes in your chosen path. However, it is not bad. Uranus wants innovation and technology, a new perspective in your career, while Saturn wants you to be disciplined about your work and routine. Try to integrate the two.

But not everything is so heavy and serious. Jupiter, the planet of expansion, opportunities, and luck is moving into the house of love and happiness. This is the 5th house which is, of course, your house as you are the 5th sign. This is great news for you. 2019 can bring happiness, love, romance, fun, and a great deal of creativity. This happens every 12 years. Go back to 2007 and 1995 and try to identify any signs of expansion in your life to predict what will take place in 2019.

Having Jupiter in Sagittarius, a fellow Fire-Bender, is very auspicious. The additional fire will bring you a boost of energy and flow. The combination of Saturn in your house of work and Jupiter in your house of fun and creativity could be linked. 2019 is a great year to shift your work from chores into joy. 2019 is a good year to change your work or shift it towards a more creative endeavor. Since the 5th house is also the house of sports and hobbies, it is a good time to engage in a new recreational activity which Saturn eventually could help you implement into your work. Who knows? Maybe while focusing on a hobby you might meet someone that will offer you a better job.

From December, Jupiter will move into Capricorn and help you start 2020 with a promotion in work, a new job offer, and better health.

Since you are a Leo, the nobility of the zodiac but also the child, having Jupiter in your house of children this year can bring a great deal of creative baby projects or even a real baby or a child into your life. Not to mention, as the title of the book suggests, this is the year everyone needs to connect to their inner child, which is always very alive in you.

The 5 Eclipses –
Your Emotional Landscape

Eclipses quicken processes and push events towards completion. They are wild-cards, amplifiers of whatever is happening in your life. They also weave stories through an endless magical tapestry of synchronicities and dreams. The eclipses this year are shifting into Cancer and Capricorn and since the North Node is in Cancer it asks us to focus on our feelings, security, compassion, and family. The Nodes represent the junction between the paths of the sun and the moon, the conjunction of the father and mother's influence. The North Node, also dubbed the Head of the Dragon, represents what our soul desires. The South Node, which is in the opposite side of the zodiac, hence in Capricorn, represents what our soul desires to let go. That means we must shed the dark side of Capricorn: fear, ignorance, lack of tolerance, fixation to the status quo, conservatism, and nationalism. Fear is partly designed to ensure our survival but being over preoccupied with ourselves and our survival can hamper the ability to see and relate to others. That is where Cancer comes in and teaches us compassion and empathy.

The eclipses this year in January, July, and December will bring us opportunities to face our fears, confront the devil, and come out winning using the magic of compassion, unconditional love and loving-kindness.

As you already know, having the North Node move away from your sign is not too bad. You can breathe deeper and relax a bit, well, at least for 19 years. However, the eclipses being in Cancer and Capricorn could make you feel a push and pull between home and career, feelings and responsibilities, mother and father, withdrawal and exposure. The eclipses can bring a great deal of fears and insecurities from early childhood and, as a Leo, the inner child in you is very dominant. But during the eclipses, the inner child can transform into inner-childishness. Since your paradox is about serving versus letting go and retreating, in the dates below the tension will be stronger between the two forces. Be especially careful around mid-July as the eclipses will combine their influence with that of Mercury retrograde, creating extra pressure and blowups.

January 5–6: Partial Solar Eclipse in Capricorn. This New Moon can activate your house of work and service but also health. Whatever is happening in your workspace is accelerated.

January 20–21: Total Lunar Eclipse Leo/Cancer cusp. This full moon takes place right on the border between Cancer and your own sign, Leo. This is the last tail of the eclipses that took place in your sign in 2017–2018. The eclipses fall on your rising sign. For this reason, it can be a bit tricky with your health and body. Take extra care. Lunar eclipses represent oppositions. In this case, it is pitting home and family opposite to career, mother versus father, your needs and your community's needs. But since it is located between the house of your body and the house of letting go, it is a good time for a cleanse or a spiritual retreat. This lunar eclipse can be especially emotional.

July 2, 2019: Total Solar Eclipse Cancer. This new moon marks a new beginning in your family life or emotional space. The key phrase here is "I feel!" Good time to start a family and make a move to a new location. The eclipse is falling in your house of mysticism, letting go, past lifetimes, and imagination. It is a great time to begin any spiritual practice that can help you tap into memories and skills from previous lives. You might go to a place or meet someone you knew in past lives.

July 16–17, 2019: Partial Lunar Eclipse Capricorn. This full moon in Capricorn once again pits career versus home and family, mother figures versus father figures. You can see that this is a recurring theme of the year. In your sign's chart, it falls between the house of work/health and the house of letting go. Another good time for a cleanse or letting go of something that blocks you in your work or health. You can also use creative visualization to manifest change in your health and professional life.

December 26, 2019: Annular Solar Eclipse Capricorn. This new moon in Capricorn falls in your house of work and health joining Saturn, Pluto, as well as Jupiter. A great deal of action and new beginning even if it is the end of the year and holidays. The key phrase is "I Use." Try to use whatever resources you have in order to manifest new aspects in your work and routine.

Mercury Retrograde – Mental Landscape

During Mercury retrograde, it is not recommended to start new long-term projects, sign documents, make large purchases, get married, publish, start marketing campaigns, or release new products. Computers crash; stock markets turn volatile; flights are delayed; traffic is worse than usual; accidents occur more often; and Murphy's Law takes hold of our lives. For example, the infamous Flash Crash of May 6, 2010, took place during Mercury retrograde in Taurus (the sign of money and the stock market). If you need to fly during Mercury retro, make sure you do your online check-in and take longer to reach the airport. Try to avoid overscheduling yourself or being overcritical and demanding. Also pay attention to your diet and food intake.

If you must start a new project, be as mindful as you can. Pay attention to small details and read in-between the lines if you must sign a document. Rewrite your emails, edit your texts, and think before you speak. In fact, it is better if you spend more time listening than talking. Life does not come to a halt during Mercury retrograde. You can still achieve a great deal. Mercury retro is like going on a vacation while it is raining. It is still possible but not much fun. However, it is a great time to edit, redo, reexamine yourself and your path, revisit old projects, and find lost objects. It is said that there are more coincidences and synchronicities while Mercury is retrograding. Try to focus on activities that have the prefix re – reevaluate, reedit, redo, reexamine, reconnect, regenerate, revisit, re-imagine, etc.

This year, Mercury is retrograding in water signs. Because you belong to the fire clan, it might be a bit more challenging as water and fire do not mix well. This combination can create steam which translates to overthinking. The retrograde from July 7-19 will be in your sign and that means you will experience more of Mercury's tricks. Be extra careful with your health and how you present yourself.

Between March 5 and March 28, Mercury retrogrades in Pisces, which falls in your house of sexuality, death, and transformation. This can be a bit intense. Mercury is the guide of the dead and for this reason you might experience more connections to dead ancestors or a better ability to connect to your intuition. However, if you have a secret love affair, it might be exposed. There will be miscommunication with investments, productions, and inheritance.

Between July 7 and July 31, Mercury retrogrades in your sign (until July 19) and then moves to Cancer shifting the confusion from your house of body and self into the house of letting go and past lives. Take extra care of your body and health. However, the retrograde can generate wild dreams, even prophecies. Your meditations could be deeper with a great deal of wisdom downloaded.

Between October 31 and November 20, Mercury retrogrades in Scorpio in your house of home and family. Miscommunications and challenges with family members, real estate, and land. This retro is especially emotional as it also creates a square in your chart, conflicts with people that are emotionally connected to you but also a call for action to fix stale relationships.

 Unpredictability, Originality and a Touch of Chaos

In May 2018, Uranus moved into Taurus and will stay there until 2026, transiting in your house of career, father figures, and bosses. Uranus is called "the Joker" or "the Fool." He is chaotic but also ingenious. You might suddenly get an "aha" moment that can help your career or professional life. Even if some of these brilliant, crazy, innovative ideas cannot manifest right now, write them down. In the future, you will find a time to bring them into fruition. However, due to Uranus' retrograde motion, he reentered your house of travel from November 7, 2018 and will be there until March 6, 2019. This means that for the first two months of the year, Uranus will be creating a bit more chaos with travel, education, publishing, and your in-laws.

Uranus favors technology, innovation, and science. Maybe you can think of a great new application or an e-commerce business. It is a good time to integrate innovation in your career. It is also a good time to redo your website, give your Facebook page a face lift, and connect to social media to promote your vocation. Be careful not to be a rebel without a cause in your career. You might find your bosses and father figures acting very crazy.

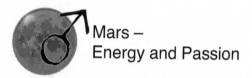

Mars – Energy and Passion

Mars governs vegetation, action, leadership, passion, and aggression. Whenever he is transiting in your sign, you feel extra energy, enthusiasm, and passion with a strong sense of purpose. Sometimes it can feel as if you are high on caffeine or even something stronger. Mars can be pushy and make you say, do, or write impulsively, giving you extra confidence that can backfire.

This year, Mars will be in your sign between July 1 and August 18. This aspect will allow you to push many projects forward and liberate you from oppressive situations. It is a great time to start a new exercise regime and assume a leadership role. However, in the first half of July, be extra careful as you have Mercury retrograde in your sign as well as an eclipse.

Below is a list of Mars' transits through the signs that can help you determine where to focus your energy. However, remember that even the best fighters need a general. Make sure you pace yourself and control your inner warrior.

 January 1 to Feb 14

You might feel aggressive but also powerful enough to manifest your wishes. This is a good time to exercise or find a new physical activity that can improve your health. Mars is transiting in your house of travel and education and can push forward an opportunity for travel or teaching.

 February 14 to March 31

This transit can help you boost your finances. It is a good time to invest in your talent and express your gifts as well as stand up for your values. Mars is transiting in your house of career and public image. It can help you assert yourself and be noticed in your work but can also cause friction with authority figures. Since Uranus and Mars will be together in Taurus, be extra careful with accidents and mishaps.

 March 31 to May 16

It is a great time for winning arguments, getting help with legal affairs, and can also provide you with an extra energy in business and writing. Be careful of fights with relatives, roommates, siblings, or neighbors. Since Mars is transiting in your house of people and friends, he can help you take a leadership role in your company, but be careful of strife with friends.

 May 16 to July 1

Good time to renovate your home, office or workspace. This Mars location can cause unnecessary conflict with your family. Since Mars is traveling in your house of letting go, he can create more interest and action with mystical pursuits. Dreams and meditation can be very vivid. Mars will help you ride the dragon (North Node in Cancer) and help you act upon your intuition.

 July 1 to August 18

Romance! A wonderful time for recreational activities, sports, hobbies, and fun. You might feel a need to engage in risky endeavors so take heed of implosive behaviors. Love is in the air as well as creativity. This aspect in the Tarot card is called Courage. Since Mars is in your house of body and personality, you might come across as aggressive and pushy, but you will feel the need to lead and take charge.

 August 18 to October 4

This time can provide extra energy and passion in your work, as well as help you find a new way to serve. A great time for diet and changes of routine. Be careful of arguments and fights with employees and coworkers. Since Mars is in your house of money, be careful of impulsiveness with finances. Talents in leadership may come to the front.

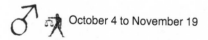 October 4 to November 19

A great time for projects with partners. Be careful of lawsuits or conflict with enemies. You might find yourself needing to spend more time or energy with partners in work or in life. Mars in your house of communication can cause you to initiate verbal fights. There could be some strife with contracts as well as relatives.

 November 19 to January 2, 2020

This is a powerful transit for Mars. Your passion, sexuality, and interest in intimacy is heightened. You will feel attractive and be able to attract opportunities in finance, investments, and production. Be careful of fights and aggressiveness with family members.

Venus: Money and Love

Venus is the ruler of pleasure, luxury, finance, talents, values, art, and relationships. She is also associated with Maat, the goddess of justice and law. Venus works in beauty cycles: the more you love yourself, the more you believe in yourself. The better your self-image, the more you connect to your talents. The more you develop and invest in your talents, the more money you can make. Venus' message is: love yourself and money will follow.

This year, the goddess of beauty will be in your sign between July 28 to August 21, making you more attractive, helping you get a raise or tap into a new talent. It is a great time for romance, making money, and connecting to your artistic side. This is a good time for you to rebrand yourself, dress differently, change your hair, or get some new clothes. Not a bad time to indulge and pamper yourself (if it is healthy and does not harm you or anyone else). This year, Mars and Venus will join together in your sign which will be a very powerful time in romance and finance between July 28 and August 18.

Conclusion:

2019 is the year where you must focus your attention on work, service, health, and diet. However, with luck and fortune moving into your house of children, creativity, and love, you might be able to wed work and happiness. Make changes in your work and routine that can bring in more joy in your life. It is a year to also focus on retreats, listening to your intuition, and setting time for yourself to be alone. Try to balance serving yourself with serving others.

23RD AUGUST – 22ND SEPTEMBER

VIRGO ♍

*When I'm feeling sad, I simply remember my favorite things, and then I don't feel so bad**

key phrase
I SERVE

element
Mutable (changeable) earth

planet
Mercury

day
Wednesday

incentive
Making things happen

body parts
Intestines, colon

color
Yellow-green

stone
Agate

---

* The Sound of Music, 1959.

I SERVE CREATIVITY.

 ## 2019 Integration: Children and friends

2019 continues your journey in the realm of love, happiness, and children. You are done being everyone's accountant. You are finished with being the editor and hiding behind the scenes. This is your year to become the star, to be on the stage and learn how to be served. Since this year is declared the year of birthing your inner child, the transits of Saturn, Pluto, the eclipses, and Jupiter will facilitate this process. You no longer need to be the super-nanny or super- manny. You can become the child.

For the last 12 months, you have been dealing with questions such as: where is my love? Where is my happiness? What makes my heart smile? How can I tap into my creativity? For some of you Virgos, it is a time to change your relationship with your children, whether they are your human kids or baby projects. With 2019's stellium in your house of children and this year being the year of birthing, you are more than ready to give birth to something huge in your life. But as always, you will do it in the quiet and humble way you are used to doing everything else. No drama, just practical, efficient, and effective giving of light.

Saturn, the Lord Karma, the rectifier according to Kabbalah, continues his journey through your house of love, happiness, and sports. For this reason, 2019 is a great time to focus and put a great deal of discipline, time, and effort in connection to a new hobby or physical activity. I know for a Virgo it might sound puerile and silly but look at it as an investment in your inner child. Eventually this investment in yourself can become pragmatic and practical. Try to travel back in time to your puberty and see if there was a subject in school that fascinated you or that you excelled in, or maybe an extra-curricular activity you later abandoned, and see if you can give your inner child some of what he/she has lost.

Since Saturn is in your house of love, he can present a potential lover but with some challenges attached. Maybe the potential lover is not available or suddenly has to move out of town for work. Don't get discouraged. Saturn is testing to see how serious and persistent you are. From December, when Jupiter enters your house of love for the entirety of 2020, romance will become easier.

As a Virgo, you like hard work. Well, hard work is coming. Your job this year is to find a way to bring creativity and happiness into your work, to find a way to let the child in you do the work, or maybe to work more with children or childlike people.

Saturn is in your house of risky endeavors so be a bit more conservative with gambling, trading, or the stock market.

Your paradox this year is whether to focus on your love, your children and your creativity, or to put your attention on your friends and community. On one hand, you have Saturn and other transits telling you that your lessons are about finding love, being creative, and connecting to your inner child. On the other hand, the South Node in the house of children tells you to let go of childish behaviors, stop thinking of your love and creativity, and focus instead on your duty towards your community or company. Should I focus on my children or other people's children? Should I focus on my creativity or support other people's projects? This year you will have to do both. Yes, let go of the childish attitude in you, but do connect to the childlike qualities.

However, not everything is so difficult. After all, we have Jupiter to bestow gifts on us. This year, Jupiter, the planet of opportunities and expansion, is moving into your house of home and family. If you ever wanted to make a move, buy a property, invest in real estate, move in with someone, or even give birth or create a family, 2019 is your year. The next 12 months are great for healing familial relationships as well as healing childhood wounds. In addition, Jupiter in Sagittarius will be squaring your sun this year. It is not an easy aspect which can come across as overconfidence or conflict with people around you. Be careful not to be full of yourself and make sure to have your ego under surveillance.

The North Node and the eclipses are moving to Cancer and Capricorn, and both signs are easy for you to handle. Uranus is also traveling in an earth sign (Taurus) which is very compatible. As a mutable earth sign, all these planets in earth and water give you an energetic boost. This means that 2019 can present you with a comfortable climate to grow into your true self.

Just remember Saturn is trying to teach you to connect to your happiness. It won't be a bad idea to invest some time in reading or learning about Positive Psychology. As a sign of service, your exploration of the importance of happiness is not for you alone to be happy but to help others tap into the spring of joy.

 ## The 5 Eclipses –
Your Emotional Landscape

Eclipses quicken processes and push events towards completion. They are wild-cards, amplifiers of whatever is happening in your life. They also weave stories through an endless magical tapestry of synchronicities and dreams. The eclipses this year are shifting into

Cancer and Capricorn and since the North Node is in Cancer it asks us to focus on our feelings, security, compassion, and family. The Nodes represent the junction between the paths of the sun and the moon, the conjunction of the father and mother's influence. The North Node, also dubbed the Head of the Dragon, represents what our soul desires. The South Node, which is in the opposite side of the zodiac, hence in Capricorn, represents what our soul desires to let go. That means we must shed the dark side of Capricorn: fear, ignorance, lack of tolerance, fixation to the status quo, conservatism, and nationalism. Fear is partly designed to ensure our survival but being over preoccupied with ourselves and our survival can hamper the ability to see and relate to others. That is where Cancer comes in and teaches us compassion and empathy.

The eclipses this year in January, July, and December will bring us opportunities to face our fears, confront the devil, and come out winning using the magic of compassion, unconditional love and loving-kindness.

As I suggested earlier, the eclipses being in Cancer and Capricorn are in earth and water signs, which are compatible with you and therefore can be easier to handle. During the eclipses, you will feel the push and pull between home and career, feelings and responsibilities, mother and father, withdrawal and exposure. However, specifically for you, the eclipses fall in your houses of children, love, and happiness, as well as the house of community. This can cause an opposition, as we saw earlier, between your children and your friends, or between your lovers and colleagues. If you are in love, or recently have a newborn, don't neglect your friends or community.

January 5–6: Partial Solar Eclipse in Capricorn. This New Moon in Capricorn falls in your house children, love, and happiness. The eclipse can serve as a focal point for Saturn's lessons of the year. Many of you Virgos will find that this eclipse can be the birthdate of your inner child.

January 20–21: Total Lunar Eclipse Leo/Cancer cusp. This full moon takes place right on the border between Cancer and Leo and falls between your houses of friends and letting go. Lunar eclipses represent oppositions. In this case, it is pitting home and family opposite to career, mother versus father, your needs and your community's needs. This lunar eclipse can also help you let go of certain friends, organizations, and change your standing in your community.

July 2, 2019: Total Solar Eclipse Cancer. The key phrase here is "I feel!" Good time to start a family and make a move to a new location. This eclipse falls in your house of friends and could bring a new affiliation to a group, a new friend, or a new network.

July 16–17, 2019: Partial Lunar Eclipse Capricorn. This full moon in Capricorn again pits career versus home and family, mother figures versus father figures. You can see that this is a recurring theme of the year. In your case, the eclipse again pits love versus friendship, or maybe children, opposite to your freedom.

December 26, 2019: Annular Solar Eclipse Capricorn. This new moon in Capricorn falls in your house of children and love joining Pluto, Saturn, as well as Jupiter. A great deal of action and new beginning even if it is the end of the year and holidays. The key phrase is "I Use." Try to use whatever resources you have to manifest new aspects with your creativity.

 Mercury Retrograde – Mental Landscape

During Mercury retrograde, it is not recommended to start new long-term projects, sign documents, make large purchases, get married, publish, start marketing campaigns, or release new products. Communications of all sorts are slower and filled with glitches and challenges. Computers crash; stock markets turn volatile; flights are delayed; traffic is worse than usual; accidents occur more often; and Murphy's Law takes hold of our lives. For example, the infamous Flash Crash of May 6, 2010, took place during Mercury retrograde in Taurus (the sign of money and the stock market). If you need to fly during Mercury retro, make sure you do your online check-in and take longer to reach the airport. Try to avoid overscheduling yourself or being overcritical and demanding. Also pay attention to your diet and food intake.

If you must start a new project, be as mindful as you can. Pay attention to small details and read in-between the lines if you must sign a document. Rewrite your emails, edit your texts, and think before you speak. In fact, it is better if you spend more time listening than talking. Life does not come to a halt during Mercury retrograde. You can still achieve a great deal. Mercury retro is like going on a vacation while it is raining. It is still possible but not much fun. However, it is a great time to edit, redo, reexamine yourself and your path, revisit old projects, and find lost objects. It is said that there are more coincidences and synchronicities during Mercury is retrograding. Try to focus on activities that have the prefix re – reevaluate, reedit, redo, reexamine, reconnect, regenerate, revisit, re-imagine, etc.

This year, Mercury is retrograding in water signs. Because you belong to the earth clan, it might not be as challenging for you since water and earth mix well together. The one retrograde that could turn out to be more difficult is between July 7–19 when Mercury will retrograde in your house of pain and suffering. In addition, this retro will be happening while the eclipse of mid-July takes place.

Between March 5 and March 28, Mercury retrogrades in Pisces, which falls in your house of relationships and marriage. This can create a great deal of miscommunications and glitches with business partners as well as your significant others. This aspect can lead to breakups.

Between July 7 and July 31, Mercury retrogrades in Leo and then moves to Cancer shifting the confusion from your house of past lifetime and letting go as well as the house of community. This retrograde can be emotional and more difficult. It can bring about lack of boundaries, hidden agendas revealed, relapses of addictions, and miscommunications with friends or colleagues.

Between October 31 and November 20, Mercury retrogrades in Scorpio in your house of communication, relatives, and contracts. You can expect issues when dealing with inheritance, other people's money, investments, taxes, and insurance. Since Mercury is the communicator and is now in your house of communication, this transit can be a bit more intense. Be careful not to be like a Scorpio and sting with your words or actions.

Unpredictability, Originality and a Touch of Chaos

In May 2018, Uranus moved into Taurus, a fellow Earth-Bender, and will stay there until 2026, falling in your house of travel, education, truth, and philosophy. Uranus might unexpectedly peak your interest in studying something to do with technology, futurism, innovation, science, or any topic you never thought will be interested in learning. Uranus is called "the Joker" or "the Fool." It is chaotic but also ingenious. You might meet foreigners or teachers that would make you see life in a different light, change your outlook on what you believe, and introduce you to new philosophies. You might suddenly get "aha" moments that can help you better understand your truth and creed. You might show a sudden interest in a new language or a new culture. Since Uranus is also transiting the house of in-laws, there might be some unexpected disruption with in-laws or some chaos with extended family.

However, due to Uranus' retrograde motion, he reentered your house of sexuality and death November 7, 2018 and will be there until March 6, 2019. This means that for the first two months of the year, Uranus will be creating a bit more chaos with your sexuality, investments, as well as in your intimate relationships. Uranus might inspire you to take a jump and a leap of faith into something totally new regarding your passion, sexuality, or joint artistic and financial affairs. An unexpected talented person might come into your life or a unique original investment.

Uranus favors technology, innovation, and science. It is also a good time to redo your website, give your Facebook page a face lift, and connect to social media.

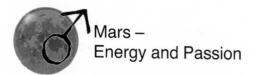# Mars – Energy and Passion

Mars governs vegetation, action, leadership, passion, and aggression. Whenever he is transiting in your sign, you feel extra energy, enthusiasm, and passion with a strong sense of purpose. Sometimes it can feel as if you are high on caffeine or even something stronger. Mars can be pushy and make you say, do, or write impulsively, giving you extra confidence that can backfire.

This year, Mars will be in your sign between August 18 and October 4. This aspect will allow you to push many projects forward and liberate you from oppressive situations. It is a great time to start a new exercise regime and assume a leadership role.

Below is a list of Mars' transits through the signs that can help you determine where to focus your energy. However, remember that even the best fighters need a general. Make sure you pace yourself and control your inner warrior.

  January 1 to Feb 14

You might feel aggressive but also powerful enough to manifest your wishes. This is a good time to exercise or find a new physical activity that can improve your health. Since Mars is transiting in your house of sexuality, your passion and intimacy is heightened. You will feel attractive and be able to attract opportunities in finance, investments, and production. Your own healing abilities can grow as well as the ability to help other people tap into their talents and finances.

 February 14 to March 31

This transit can help you boost your finances. It is a good time to invest in your talents and express your gifts as well as stand up for your values. This transit of Mars falls in your house of travel and education. A great time for adventures and embarking on a journey to a place you have never visited either physically (traveling) or mentally (through study). It is a time to fight for your truth. Some conflict can take place with in-laws. Since Mars and Uranus are coming together, be careful of accidents and mishaps.

  March 31 to May 16

It is a great time for winning arguments, getting help with legal affairs, and can also provide you with an extra energy in business and writing. Be careful of fights with relatives, roommates, siblings, or neighbors. This transit of Mars takes place in your house of career. It is a good time to assert yourself and ask for a promotion or assume a leadership role. Be careful of conflicts with bosses, father figures, or competitive colleges.

 May 16 to July 1

Good time to renovate your home, office or workspace. This Mars location can cause unnecessary conflict with your family. Mars falls in your house of community, friends, companies, and clubs. You will feel extra competitive with people in your group of friends or company. It is a good time for team sports or any activity that involves a community. Be careful of fights or politics in your company. Mars can give you the energy you need to ride the Dragon (North Node in Cancer) and get a promotion in your company.

 July 1 to August 18

A wonderful time for recreational activities, sports, hobbies, and fun. You might feel a need to engage in risky endeavors so take heed of implosive behaviors. Love is in the air as well as creativity. This transit takes place in your house of letting go, past lifetimes, hidden enemies, hospitals, jails, and confinement. Be extra careful of injuries or accidents that can lead to a visit to the ER. You also must be aware that you might make hidden enemies. Memories from past lives might return as well as meetings with people you have known in previous lives.

 August 18 to October 4

This time can provide extra energy and passion in your work, as well as help you find a new way to serve. A great time for diet and changes of routine. Be careful of arguments and fights with employees and coworkers. Since Mars is transiting in your own sign, you will feel like a superhero with extra energy and vitality. Don't over extend yourself or over train.

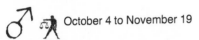 October 4 to November 19

A great time for projects with partners. Be careful of lawsuits or conflict with enemies. You might find yourself needing to spend more time or energy with partners in work or in life. This transit can help you make a push in your finances. It is a time to invest in your talents and express your gifts as well as stand up for your values. Be careful not to spend too much money or be impulsively generous to the wrong people.

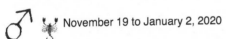 November 19 to January 2, 2020

This is a powerful transit for Mars. Your passion, sexuality, and interest in intimacy is heightened. You will feel attractive and be able to attract opportunities in finance, investments, and production. Your own healing abilities can grow as well as the ability to help other people tap into their talents and finance. Like in the case of the last Mercury retrograde we mentioned earlier, take care not to be too strong in your communication or overly critical. However, since Mars is in your third house, it is great for winning arguments, legal affairs, and extra energy in business and writing. Be careful of fights with relatives, siblings, roommates, or neighbors. Your communication can cause conflict but also move mountains. Good for sales and marketing.

Venus: Money and Love

Venus is the ruler of pleasure, luxury, finance, talents, values, art, and relationships. She is also associated with Maat, the goddess of justice and law. Venus works in beauty cycles: the more you love yourself, the more you believe in yourself. The better your self-image, the more you connect to your talents. The more you develop and invest in your talents, the more money you can make. Venus' message is: love yourself and money will follow.

This year, the goddess of beauty will be in your sign between August 21 and September 14, making you more attractive, helping you get a raise, or tap into a new talent. It is a great time for romance, making money, and connecting to your artistic side. This is a good time for you to rebrand yourself, dress differently, change your hair, or get some new clothes. Not a bad time to indulge and pamper yourself (if it is healthy and does not harm you or anyone else).

This year you are lucky! Mars and Venus will be spending time together in your sign between August 21 to September 14. This will help you with passion, finance and love.

Conclusion:

Overall, most of the transits this year (Pluto, Saturn, Uranus, North Nodes) are helping you achieve the most of 2019. Since Saturn and the eclipses are helping you better understand the concept of love, creativity, and children, 2019 is indeed a great year to give birth to your inner child, baby project, and of course real babies. You must remember not to abandon your friends and communities as you discover your own creativity and love.

23RD SEPTEMBER – 22ND OCTOBER

LIBRA

*Country roads, take me home, to the place I belong**

key phrase
I BALANCE

element
Cardinal air

planet
Venus

day
Friday

incentive
Mirror of love affairs

body parts
Kidneys, waist, ovaries

color
Green

stone
Opal

---

* John Denver, 1971.

I BALANCE HOME AND CAREER.

 ## 2019 Integration: Personal and professional life

2019 continues your journey to heal, focus, rectify, and restructure your home and family life. Saturn, the Lord Karma, the grand teacher and the rectifier, is helping you rebuild your abode, your shell, your temple. Once in 28 years, Saturn returns to the foundation of your chart and cleans your cellars. When Saturn is transiting in the lowest part of your chart, he is helping you cleanse deep-rooted emotional issues dating back either 28 years and/or to early childhood. This means that things you have been sweeping under the carpet for decades are resurfacing and demand conformation and healing. You have already been working hard on creating a family for a year, fixing your habitat, changing homes, dealing with family members, and focusing on the key phrase, "I feel." Even your relationships with your mother and mother figures were and are going through an adjustment. Since Libra is the sign of relationships, having Saturn in the house of home is helping you understand the connection between conditioning done in your early childhood and your current significant relationships. This is also true since Chiron, the wounded healer, has moved to your house of relationships, bringing into the open ancient wounds that afflict all your partnerships in work or in life.

Saturn is also transiting in your house of the "end of things," helping you get resolutions and completion. 2019 is a good year to close circles, end cycles, and bring things to an end, which perfectly fits the energies of the number 12 associated with this year. This year, you can break patterns that have been causing you to live in circles.

Since the North Node is in Cancer, the sign of home and family, it is asking you to learn the lessons of forgiveness and compassion. As you can see, there is a planetary convergence in 2019 helping you fix the home front as well as increase your emotional intelligence. This will be especially powerful in December, when Jupiter will enter your house of home providing opportunities to buy property, renovate a home, move to a better place, or start a family.

To resolve your 2019 paradox, you will need to pull out your famous scales of justice and your gift for compromises. While it is true that you have a convergence of planets and aspects in your house of home and family (Saturn, Pluto, north node in Cancer, 3 eclipses), what your soul desires is to work on your career and thus let go of your focus on home. How is it possible? The North Node always tells us where we need to focus our attention to grow, and indeed it is in Cancer, the sign that rules homes and family. However, in your case, it is located this year in your house of career, which means that to succeed in your career, you need to let go of home. But we just agreed that you need to focus on home. 2019 is your time to integrate home and career. Maybe find a way to work from home part of the time or find a workplace that feels like home.

Jupiter, the planet of expansion and luck, is now transiting in your house of communication, contracts, relatives, and writing. This year, you will feel an urge or need to write and publish. You might find your ability to communicate improves dramatically as well as your ability to relate to people and become a connector, a hub. Since you are a cardinal air sign, you are the leader of communication in the zodiac and having Jupiter in the house of communication will give you a boost. Since Jupiter is also blessing your house of relatives, siblings, roommates, and neighbors, these people might help you or you will find the relationship with them improve.

The combination of Jupiter in the house of siblings and communication and Saturn in the house of home can offer an opportunity to fix your relationships with your family of origin as well as your new family.

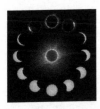

The 5 Eclipses –
Your Emotional Landscape

Eclipses quicken processes and push events towards completion. They are wild-cards, amplifiers of whatever is happening in your life. They also weave stories through an endless magical tapestry of synchronicities and dreams. The eclipses this year are shifting into Cancer and Capricorn and since the North Node is in Cancer it asks us to focus on our feelings, security, compassion, and family. The Nodes represent the junction between the paths of the sun and the moon, the conjunction of the father and mother's influence. The North Node, also dubbed the Head of the Dragon, represents what our soul desires. The South Node, which is in the opposite side of the zodiac, hence in Capricorn, represents what our soul desires to let go. That means we must shed the dark side of Capricorn: fear, ignorance, lack of tolerance, fixation on the status quo, conservatism, and nationalism. Fear is partly designed to ensure our survival but being over preoccupied with ourselves and our survival can hamper the ability to see and relate to others. That is where Cancer comes in and teaches us compassion and empathy.

The eclipses this year in January, July, and December will bring us opportunities to face our fears, confront the devil, and come out winning using the magic of compassion, unconditional love, and loving-kindness.

The eclipses being in Cancer and Capricorn, fellow Cardinal signs, can make January, July, and December a bit more emotional and challenging as you also are a Cardinal sign. In other words, the eclipses create a square to your sun. This can cause you to be very reactive and impulsive. Please take heed around the eclipses this year. During the eclipses, you will feel an especially strong the constant push and pull between home and career, feelings and reason, mother and father, withdrawal and exposure. The eclipses can bring a great deal of fears and insecurities from early childhood.

January 5–6: Partial Solar Eclipse in Capricorn. This New Moon in Capricorn falls in your house of home and family and can present opportunities to begin something new with your residence, office, car, or whatever contains you. The eclipse could bring into the light hidden memories from your childhood. Overcoming fear is one of the lessons of this eclipse.

January 20–21: Total Lunar Eclipse Leo/Cancer cusp. This full moon takes place right on the border between Cancer and Leo and falls between your houses of career and community. Lunar eclipses represent oppositions. In this case it is pitting home and family opposite to career, mother versus father, your needs and your community's needs. This lunar eclipse can be especially emotional, and it can also trigger insecurities with friends or your company.

July 2, 2019: Total Solar Eclipse Cancer. This new moon marks a new beginning in your career and professional life. The key phrase here is "I feel!" It is also a good eclipse to fix and heal issues with father figures, bosses, or people of authority.

July 16–17, 2019: Partial Lunar Eclipse Capricorn. This full moon in Capricorn again pits career versus home and family, mother figures versus father figures. You can see that this is a recurring theme of the year. You need to be more receptive to changes in home and more active in your career.

December 26, 2019: Annular Solar Eclipse Capricorn. This new moon in Capricorn falls in your house of home joining Saturn, Pluto, as well as Jupiter. A great deal of action and new beginnings even if it is the end of the year and holidays. The key phrase is "I Use." Try to use whatever resources you have in order to fix, evolve, and shift the energy with family members and home. A good time to heal and connect to a mother figure or a healer.

 ## Mercury Retrograde – Mental Landscape

During Mercury retrograde, it is not recommended to start new long-term projects, sign documents, make large purchases, get married, publish, start marketing campaigns, or release new products. Communications of all sorts are slower and filled with glitches and challenges. Computers crash; stock markets turn volatile; flights are delayed; traffic is worse than usual; accidents occur more often; and Murphy's Law takes hold of our lives. For example, the infamous Flash Crash of May 6, 2010, took place during Mercury retrograde in Taurus (the sign of money and the stock market). If you need to fly during Mercury retro, make sure you do your online check-in and take longer to reach the airport. Try to avoid overscheduling yourself or being overly critical and demanding. Also pay attention to your diet and food intake.

If you must start a new project, be as mindful as you can. Pay attention to small details and read in-between the lines if you must sign a document. Rewrite your emails; edit your texts; and think before you speak. In fact, it is better if you spend more time listening than talking. Life does not come to a halt during Mercury retrograde. You can still achieve a great deal. Mercury retro is like going on a vacation while it is raining. It is still possible but not much fun. However, it is a great time to edit, redo, reexamine yourself and your path, revisit old projects, and find lost objects. It is said that there are more coincidences and synchronicities while Mercury is retrograding. Try to focus on activities that have the prefix *re* – reevaluate, reedit, redo, reexamine, reconnect, regenerate, revisit, re-imagine, etc.

This year, Mercury is retrograding in water signs. Because you belong to the air clan, it might be a bit more challenging as water and air don't mix that well. It is like throwing your computer into the pool. As an Air-Bender, you might experience emotional moments during the retrogrades as well as bubbles that can burst.

Between March 5 and March 28, Mercury retrogrades in Pisces, which falls in your house of work, health, diet, routine, and employees. Watch your health and be extra careful with people who serve you, employees, or coworkers as you might experience a great deal of miscommunications. Be careful of relapses with any substances or drugs and watch your diet.

Between July 7 and July 31, Mercury retrogrades in Leo and then moves to Cancer, shifting the confusion from your house of friends and company to the house of career. Difficulties communicating with bosses and father figures, glitches in your professional life, as well as how you deal with friends or members of your community.

Between October 31 and November 20, Mercury retrogrades in Scorpio in your house of money, talents, and self-worth. Watch your expenses and be careful not to make mistakes with your finances or your partner's money. In addition, be careful with investments.

# Unpredictability, Originality and a Touch of Chaos

In May 2018, Uranus moved into Taurus and will stay there until 2026, falling in your house of your partner's money, sexuality, intimacy, death, and transformation. Uranus is called "the Joker" or "the Fool." It is chaotic but also ingenious. You might suddenly get "aha" moments that can help you deal with other people's money and talents. Your healing abilities and intuition can increase dramatically. You will become everyone's psychic or confession booth. There could be unpredictability with your partner's finance, whether it is a business or a love partner. Maybe an unexpected inheritance. However, Uranus being changeable, this aspect can also manifest as an unforeseen parting or death (symbolic or real).

Due to Uranus' retrograde motion, he reentered your opposite sign, Aries, in November 7, 2018 and will be there until March 6, 2019. This means that, for the first two months of the year, Uranus will be creating a bit more chaos with your house of relationships and partnerships. But hey, you should be used to it as it has been like this since 2010.

From March 6, Uranus might inspire you to take a leap of faith into something totally new regarding your healing abilities, your intimacy and sexuality, as well as joint artistic and financial affairs. After all, Uranus is now transiting in the house of occult and magic, connecting you to the ability to manifest your desires or other people's wishes. You are a wizard!

Uranus favors technology, innovation, and science. Maybe you can think of a great new application or an e-commerce business, especially if it involves an investor or collaborating with other people.

Good aspect for investment in technology, e-commerce, and start-ups.

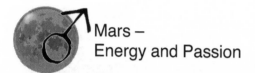

Mars –
Energy and Passion

Mars governs vegetation, action, leadership, passion, and aggression. Whenever he is transiting in your sign, you feel extra energy, enthusiasm, passion, and a strong sense of purpose. Mars can help you plant new seeds in the ground as well as empower whatever you are passionate about. Sometimes it can feel as if you are high on caffeine or even something stronger. Mars can be pushy and make you say, do, or write impulsively, giving you extra confidence that can backfire.

This year, Mars will be in your sign between October 4 and November 19. This aspect will allow you to push many projects forward and liberate you from oppressive situations. It is a great time to start a new exercise regime and assume a leadership role.

Below is a list of Mars' transits through the signs that can help you determine where to focus your energy. However, remember that even the best fighters need a general. Make sure you pace yourself and control your inner warrior.

 January 1 to Feb 14

You might feel aggressive but also powerful enough to manifest your wishes. This is a good time to exercise or find a new physical activity that can improve your health. Mars is transiting in your house of relationships; therefore, it is great time for projects with partners. Be careful of lawsuits or conflict with enemies. This is a classic aspect of breakups. So be extra careful. It is also a time when you might embark on a crusade against your enemies.

  February 14 to March 31

This transit can help you boost your finances by working with other people's talents and money. Mars is transiting in your house of sexuality. This is a powerful transit for Mars. Your passion, sexuality, and intimacy are heightened. You will feel attractive and be able to attract opportunities in finance, investments, and production. Your own healing abilities can grow as well as the ability to help other people tap into their true potential. Since Mars and Uranus will be in conjunction, it can cause accidents and mishaps. Be extra careful.

  March 31 to May 16

It is a great time for winning arguments, getting help with legal affairs, and can also provide you with extra energy in business and writing. Be careful of fights with relatives, roommates, siblings, or neighbors. This transit of Mars falls in your house of travel and education. A great time for adventures and embarking on a journey to a place you have never visited either physically (traveling) or mentally (through study). It is a time to fight for your truth. Some conflict can take place with in-laws.

 May 16 to July 1

Good time to renovate your home, office, or workspace. This Mars location can cause unnecessary conflict with your family. This transit of Mars takes place in your house of career. It is a good time to assert yourself and ask for a promotion or assume a leadership role. Be careful of conflicts with bosses, father figures, or competitive colleagues. You can ride the dragon (North Node in Cancer) towards a better career and success in your professional life.

 July 1 to August 18

A wonderful time for recreational activities, sports, hobbies, and fun. You might feel a need to engage in risky endeavors so take heed with implosive behaviors. Love is in the air as well as creativity. Mars falls in your house of community, friends, companies, and clubs. You will feel extra competitive with people in your group of friends or company. It is a good time for team sports or any activity that involves a community. Be careful of fights or politics in your company.

 August 18 to October 4

This time can provide extra energy and passion in your work, as well as help you find a new way to serve. A great time for diet and changes of routine. Be careful of arguments and fights with employees and coworkers. Be extra careful of injuries, inflammations, and stress. This transit takes place in your house of letting go, past lifetimes, hidden enemies, hospitals, jails, and confinement. Be extra careful of injuries or accidents that can lead to a visit to the ER. You also must be aware that you might make hidden enemies. Memories from past lives might return as well as meetings with people you have known in past lives.

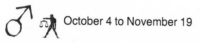 October 4 to November 19

A great time for projects with partners. Be careful of lawsuits or conflict with enemies. You might find yourself needing to spend more time or energy with partners in work or in life. This transit takes place in your sign and therefore in your house of your body and personality. You might feel aggressive but also powerful enough to manifest your wishes. This is a good time to exercise or find a new physical activity that can improve your health. Be careful not to be at war with yourself.

 November 19 to January 2, 2020

This is a powerful transit for Mars. Your passion, sexuality, and interest in intimacy is heightened. You will feel attractive and be able to attract opportunities in finance, investments, and production. This transit can help you make a push in your finances. It is a time to invest in your talents and express your gifts as well as stand up for your values. Be careful not to spend too much money or be impulsively generous to the wrong people.

 # Venus: Money and Love

Venus, the ruler of your sign, is the planet the governs pleasure, luxury, finance, talents, values, art, and relationships. She is also associated with Maat, the goddess of justice and law. That is why she is your ruler, as you are the sign of the scales. Venus works in beauty cycles: the more you love yourself, the more you believe in yourself. The better your self-image, the more you connect to your talents. The more you develop and invest in your talents, the more money you can make. Venus' message is: love yourself and money will follow.

This year, the goddess of beauty will be in your sign between September 14 and October 8, making you more attractive, helping you get a raise or tap into a new talent. It is a great time for romance, making money, and connecting to your artistic side. This is a good time for you to rebrand yourself, dress differently, change your hair, or get some new clothes. Not a bad time to indulge and pamper yourself (if it is healthy and does not harm you or anyone else). This year, you are one of the only 3 signs that will have the honor to host Mars and Venus together in your sign. This will take place between October 4 – 8. It is a great time for romance, improve your finance and connect to the artist in you.

Conclusion:

2019 is a paradoxical year for you Libras. It asks you to focus on home and yet instructs you to let go of your personal life so you can reconnect to your career. This year, you will have to use all your balancing acts to create an equilibrium between the need to nest and the importance of hunting, the pull towards home and the push towards your career. There will be a great deal of opportunities with new businesses, contracts, as well as writing projects and making good connections.

23RD OCTOBER – 22ND NOVEMBER

SCORPIO ♏

I feel good, I knew that I would now, so good, so good. *

key phrase
I TRANSFORM

element
Fixed (unchangeable) water

planet
Mars

day
Tuesday

incentive
Regeneration

body parts
Sex organs, reproductive system, nose

color
Turquoise/green-blue

stone
Topaz

---

* James Brown, 1964.

I TRANSFORM COMMUNICATION.

2019 Integration:
My truth versus your truth

2019 continues transforming your communication and your connection to *logos*, the word. In many traditions, the power of the word is the power of creation. In *Genesis*, Elohim said "Let there be light," and there was light. God didn't think or imagine, God said. By the same token, the magical spell *abracadabra*, means "I shall create that which I said." If Scorpio is the sign of magic, then next year you are learning how to use words, communication, letters, digits, and signs in the service of transformation.

Being a secretive sign, the archetype of the spy, someone who listens and does not talk, someone who holds the cards close, it might not be comfortable for you to focus so much attention on communication. However, when Saturn, the Lord Karma, the grand teacher and the rectifier, is in your house of communication, he forces you to look at how you relate to others as well as to create a new infrastructure of your communication. What is your message? Who do you want to deliver the message to? In 2019, you will be asked to be a connector, a mediator, someone who can translate opposing forces and build bridges. 2019 will ask you to also consider spending more time writing or, better still, change the way you usually communicate. As you are the sign of healing and therapy, it also could manifest in a newfound ability to transform people using language. If you always say "I think…" maybe you should try "I believe…" or "I feel…"

Be extra careful during the eclipses (listed below), especially during the period of July 7 to 31, where you will have Mercury retrograde and the eclipses. This can be the most challenging period of communication.

Saturn in the house of business can help you think, conjure, and manifest ideas for a new project or endeavor. Since Saturn is also in your house of marketing, you will have to learn to talk about yourself or your work and make sure you promote yourself. If you never do it, well, that's what Saturn is trying to teach you. If you did market and promote yourself before in a certain way, now it's the year to try a new form of self-promotion.

Since Saturn is transiting in your house of siblings, relatives, roommates, and neighbors, he could cause situations that will demand looking into patterns you might have with these people. Saturn is not always a bad thing. Maybe your brother has a newborn baby and you have new responsibilities or maybe a relative is moving to your city and you have to help them. Since Saturn is also in your house of contracts, you might have to rewrite and reexamine your agreements and bonds.

2019 paradox is revolving around the question: what is your truth? How is that truth relates to other people's truth? On the one hand, you have the North Node in your house of truth and philosophy. This means that you need to focus on your truth and not compromise your values and what you believe in. On the other hand, all the planets in the house of marketing, business, and communications ask you to bend the truth so you could be more successful in sales or promotion. What should you do? I think the integration should be focused on promoting and marketing, creating businesses and communicating products or ideas that you absolutely believe in and would use yourself. This year, you must walk the talk.

Jupiter, the planet of benevolence and the giver of gifts in 2019, is moving into your house of money, talents, and self-worth. This is great news for your finances as you might get a boost with your income or a raise. There could also be a new talent that you might have neglected for 12, 24, or 36 years that can resurface. You might feel better about yourself, get recognition, awards, or prizes. From December, Jupiter will move into Capricorn and will join Pluto, Saturn, and the eclipses in your house of communication. This will give you a great deal of gifts with new businesses and new connections.

 ## The 5 Eclipses – Your Emotional Landscape

Eclipses quicken processes and push events towards completion. They are wild-cards, amplifiers of whatever is happening in your life. They also weave stories through an endless magical tapestry of synchronicities and dreams. The eclipses this year are shifting into Cancer and Capricorn and since the North Node is in Cancer it asks us to focus on our feelings, security, compassion, and family. The Nodes represent the junction between the paths of the sun and the moon, the conjunction of the father and mother's influence. The North Node, also dubbed the Head of the Dragon, represents what our soul desires. The South Node, which is in the opposite side of the zodiac, hence in Capricorn, represents what our soul desires to let go. That means we must shed the dark side of Capricorn: fear, ignorance, lack of tolerance, fixation to the status quo, conservatism, and nationalism. Fear is partly designed to ensure our survival but being over preoccupied with ourselves and our survival can hamper the ability to see and relate to others. That is where Cancer comes in and teaches us compassion and empathy.

The eclipses this year in January, July, and December will bring us opportunities to face our fears, confront the devil, and come out winning using the magic of compassion, unconditional love, and loving-kindness.

The eclipses, being in Cancer and Capricorn, are a bit easier for you compare to other signs. You are a Water-Bender, and Cancer is a fellow water sign, while Capricorn is a compatible earthling. That means that you can use the eclipses to push things forward in your life. However, eclipses are eclipses and you are not immune. During the eclipses, you will feel an especially strong push and pull between home and career, feelings and responsibilities, mother and father, withdrawal versus exposure. The eclipses can bring a great deal of fears and insecurities from early childhood.

January 5–6: Partial Solar Eclipse in Capricorn. This New Moon in Capricorn falls in your house of communication, the very house Saturn is trying to fix. This is a good time to launch a new business, start a writing project, or work on communication.

January 20–21: Total Lunar Eclipse Leo/Cancer cusp. This full moon takes place right on the border between Cancer and Leo and falls between your houses of career and travel. Lunar eclipses represent oppositions. In this case, it is pitting home and family opposite to career, mother versus father, your needs and your community's needs. This lunar eclipse can be especially emotional. Since it is located in your career as well as travel, pay extra attention if you travel for your career or if you are teaching or consulting in your career.

July 2, 2019: Total Solar Eclipse Cancer. This new moon marks a new beginning in your family life or emotional space. The key phrase here is "I feel!" Good time to start a family and make a move to a new location. The eclipse falls in your house of travel so if you plan to relocate to a new country, it is a good time. Also, a good time to start a new course of study or travel.

July 16–17, 2019: Partial Lunar Eclipse Capricorn. This full moon in Capricorn once again pits career versus home and family, mother figures versus father figures. You can see that this is a recurring theme of the year. Since the eclipse is falling in your house of communication, it can trigger some miscommunications, especially since it is also during Mercury retrograde.

December 26, 2019: Annular Solar Eclipse Capricorn. This new moon in Capricorn falls in your house of communication and business joining Saturn, Pluto, as well as Jupiter. A great deal of action and new beginning even if it is the end of the year and holidays. The key phrase is "I Use." Try to use whatever resources you have to manifest new aspects in your business and marketing.

Mercury Retrograde – Mental Landscape

During Mercury retrograde, it is not recommended to start new long-term projects, sign documents, make large purchases, get married, publish, start marketing campaigns, or release new products. Communications of all sorts are slower and filled with glitches and challenges. Computers crash; stock markets turn volatile; flights are delayed; traffic is worse than usual; accidents occur more often; and Murphy's Law takes hold of our lives. For example, the infamous Flash Crash of May 6, 2010, took place during Mercury retrograde in Taurus (the sign of money and the stock market). If you need to fly during Mercury retro, make sure you do your online check-in and take longer to reach the airport. Try to avoid overscheduling yourself or being overly critical and demanding. Also pay attention to your diet and food intake.

If you must start a new project, be as mindful as you can. Pay attention to small details and read in-between the lines if you must sign a document. Rewrite your emails, edit your texts, and think before you speak. In fact, it is better if you spend more time listening than talking. Life does not come to a halt during Mercury retrograde. You can still achieve a great deal. Mercury retro is like going on a vacation while it is raining. It is still possible but not much fun. However, it is a great time to edit, redo, reexamine yourself and your path, revisit old projects, and find lost objects. It is said that there are more coincidences and synchronicities while Mercury is retrograding. Try to focus on activities that have the prefix *re* – reevaluate, reedit, redo, reexamine, reconnect, regenerate, revisit, re-imagine, etc.

This year, Mercury retrograde is especially important for you (the third one actually falls in your sign), since retrograde always causes issues in communication and this year Saturn is transiting in your house of communication.

This year, Mercury is retrograding in water signs, which is great for you being a fellow water sign. As a Water-Bender, you might experience emotional swings but also the ability to dive deep into these feelings and come out transformed.

Between March 5 and March 28, Mercury retrogrades in Pisces, which falls in your house of children, love, and creativity. If you have children, there could be a lot of misunderstanding around them or difficulty communicating. There could also be arguments with lovers or around creative projects.

Between July 7 and July 31, Mercury retrogrades in Leo and then moves to Cancer shifting the confusion from your house of travel and education to career. Miscommunication with bosses, in-laws, foreigners, and teachers can come to the front.

Between October 31 and November 20, Mercury retrogrades in you sign and therefore can affect you much more. Be extra careful how you present yourself. Remember marketing is the theme this year. Also watch your body and be careful of accidents or mishaps.

Unpredictability, Originality and a Touch of Chaos

In May 2018, Uranus moved into Taurus and will stay there until 2026, falling in your house of relationships and marriage. This is not an easy aspect as Uranus is now in your opposite sign, which means that Uranus is opposing your sun, especially if you are born the first few days of Scorpio (October 23-29). This can manifest as feeling the earth moving, sudden twists and turns, people bailing out on you, instability, and lack of consistency.

Uranus is called "the Joker" or "the Fool." It is chaotic but also ingenious. You might suddenly get an "aha" moment that can help you understand your relationships or partnerships. Since Uranus is funny, your current partner might become more humorous or you might encounter funny people who are unique, original, and spontaneous. Stale and old relationships might suddenly disappear, and new exciting ones can come into your life. You might feel like you need more freedom or your partner in work or in life will demand it.

However, due to Uranus' retrograde motion, he reentered Aries in November 7, 2018 and will stay there until March 6, 2019. This means that for the first two months of the year, Uranus will be creating a bit more chaos where it has been since 2010 in your house of work, health, diet, and service.

From March 6, Uranus might inspire you to take a leap of faith into a new partnership or a new relationship. Uranus favors technology, innovation, and science. Try to bring some innovation or spontaneity into your existing relationships. Try to do something new.

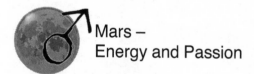

Mars –
Energy and Passion

Mars, your ruler, governs vegetation, action, leadership, passion, and aggression. Whenever he is transiting in your sign, you feel extra energy, enthusiasm, passion, and a strong sense of purpose. Sometimes it can feel as if you are high on caffeine or even something stronger. Mars can be pushy and make you say, do, or write impulsively, giving you extra confidence that can backfire.

This year, Mars, your planet, will be in your sign between November 19 and January 2, 2020. This aspect will allow you to push many projects forward and liberate you from oppressive situations. It is a great time to start a new exercise regime and assume a leadership role.

Below is a list of Mars' transits through the signs that can help you determine where to focus your energy. However, remember that even the best fighters need a general. Make sure you pace yourself and control your inner warrior.

 January 1 to Feb 14

You might feel aggressive but also the power to manifest your wishes. This is a good time to exercise or find a new physical activity that can improve your health. This transit can give you extra energy and passion in your work, as well as help you find a new way to serve. A great time for diet and changes of routine. Be careful of arguments and fights with employees and coworkers. Be extra careful of injuries, inflammations, and stress.

 February 14 to March 31

Mars is transiting opposite to your sign, but he can help with boosting your finances. It is a good time to invest in your talents and express your gifts as well as stand up for your values. Be careful not to overspend money. Mars is transiting in your house of relationships; therefore, it is a great time for projects with partners. Be careful of lawsuits or conflict with enemies. This is a classic aspect of break-ups so be extra careful. It is also a time when you might embark on a crusade against your enemies. Uranus joins Mars in this period, be extra careful with mishaps and accidents.

 March 31 to May 16

It is a great time for winning arguments, getting help with legal affairs, and can also provide you with an extra energy in business and writing. Be careful of fights with relatives, roommates, siblings, or neighbors. This is a powerful transit for Mars. Your passion, sexuality, and intimacy is heightened. You will feel attractive and be able to attract opportunities in finance, investments, and production. Your own healing abilities can grow as well as the ability to help other people tap into their talents and finances.

 May 16 to July 1

Good time to renovate your home, office or workspace. This Mars location can cause unnecessary conflict with your family. This transit of Mars falls in your house of travel and education. A great time for adventures and embarking on a journey to a place you have never visited either physically (traveling) or mentally (through study). It is a time to fight for your truth. Some conflict can take place with in-laws. Since the North Node is in Cancer, you can ride the dragon to distant lands.

 July 1 to August 18

A wonderful time for recreational activities, sports, hobbies, and fun. You might feel a need to engage in risky endeavors so take heed with implosive behaviors. Love is in the air as well as creativity. Your inner child is active but be careful of injuries. This transit of Mars takes place in your house of career. It is a good time to assert yourself and ask for a promotion or assume a leadership role. Be careful of conflicts with bosses, father figures, or competitive colleagues.

 August 18 to October 4

This time can provide extra energy and passion in your work, as well as help you find a new way to serve. A great time for diet and changes of routine. Be careful of arguments and fights with employees and coworkers. Be extra careful of injuries, inflammations, and stress. Mars falls in your house of community, friends, companies, and clubs. You will feel extra competitive with people in your group of friends or company. It is a good time for team sports or any activity that involves a community. Be careful of fights or politics in your company.

 October 4 to November 19

A great time for projects with partners. Be careful from lawsuits or conflict with enemies. You might find yourself needing to spend more time or energy with partners in work or in life. You partners might initiate fights or activate your passion. This transit takes place in your house of letting go, past lifetimes, hidden enemies, hospitals, jails, and confinement. Be extra careful from injuries or accidents that can lead to a visit to the ER. You also must be aware that you might make hidden enemies. Memories from past lives might return as well as meetings with people you have known in past lives.

 November 19 to January 2, 2020

This is a powerful transit for Mars in general and specific for you as a Scorpio. Your passion, sexuality, and interest in intimacy is heightened. You will feel attractive and be able to attract opportunities in finance, investments, and production. Your own healing abilities can grow as well as the ability to help other people tap into their talents and finance. Since this transit takes place in your house of body and personality, you might feel aggressive and need to push yourself and others forward. This is a good time to exercise, find a new physical activity, and train. Be careful not to be at war with yourself.

 ## Venus: Money and Love

Venus is the ruler of pleasure, luxury, finance, talents, values, art, and relationships. She is also associated with Maat, the goddess of justice and law. Venus works in beauty cycles: the more you love yourself, the more you believe in yourself. The better your self-image, the more you connect to your talents. The more you develop and invest in your talents, the more money you can make. Venus' message is: love yourself and money will follow.

This year, the goddess of beauty will be in your sign twice! The first seven days of the year and again between October 8 and November 1, Venus is making you more attractive, helping you get a raise or tap into a new talent. These are great times for romance, making money, and connecting to your artistic side. These are also good times for you to rebrand yourself, dress differently, change your hair, or get some new clothes. Not a bad time to indulge and pamper yourself (if it is healthy and does not harm you or anyone else).

Conclusion:

2019 is the year where you can get out of contracts that no longer serve you as well as make new connections that can bloom in the next 30 years. 2019 is the year where you are asked to change your communication as well as focus on writing, becoming a messenger, publishing, creating a network, and embarking on new businesses and projects. It is a year when you can fix your relationships with relatives as well as find new brothers and sisters in arms

23RD NOVEMBER – 21ST DECEMBER

SAGITTARIUS

I see my light come shinin' from the west unto the east, any day now, I shall be released.*

key phrase
I see: prophecy

element
Mutable (changeable) fire

planet
Jupiter

day
Thursday

incentive
Embers and torch

body parts
Liver, thighs and hips

color
Blue

stone
Turquoise

---

* Bob Dylan, 1967.

144

I SEE MY WORTH.

 ## 2019 Integration: My values versus my partner's values

2019 continues your journey into discovering your true potential, talents, and self-worth. These lessons started a long time ago. At the end of 2014, Saturn, the Lord Karma, the grand teacher, moved into your sign and started changing you inside out. You could no longer ignore your issues with your signature optimism and happy-go-lucky attitude. In December 2017, you were finally freed from Saturn and throughout 2018 you slowly recuperated and reignited your fire.

Saturn is transiting in your house money, talents, and self-worth. In 2019, you need to invest money, faith, and time in your talents. It is a great year to change the way you make money by tapping into hidden or forgotten talents that sit better with your current values, which probably changed dramatically in the last three years. Some of you will experience lower income or less money in the bank due to long-term investments in new sources of money. But with your planet, Jupiter, moving in December 2019 to your house of money, your financial situation should improve in 2020.

Saturn wants you to look into your values and be open to changing some of them. You can get preachy and stubborn with your philosophies and outlook on life. 2019 offers you an opportunity to change the ideals or philosophies that hold you back and prevent you from growing. Free your mind, the rest should follow. The change in values or outlook on life could help you tap into new talents and, with the help of improved self-worth, get you to the right path financially. Yes, you can make money from things you love.

Saturn is not the only planet in your house of finance. The eclipses in January, July, and December, can also push forward new projects and new ways of making money. In addition, the North Node, which represents what your soul desires to learn, is moving this year into your house of other people's money and talents. This means that your income can increase by co-creation or working in joint artistic or join financial projects. The North Node is also in your house of sexuality and intimacy and is trying to help you connect to your true passion. Sagittarians, you move with freedom and are addicted to thrills, but in 2019, your job is to connect your mind, heart, and sexual organs. Intimacy and sexuality are getting married this year.

This leads us to your 2019 paradox. As we saw, your job this year is to focus on your money, talents, and self-worth. However, the North Node in Cancer is telling you to let go of your own value and talents and learn to cooperate with other people's talents to help others make money. Maybe you can find your talents while you are helping others tap into their own gifts. Maybe you can change your values to fit better with other people's philosophies.

Jupiter transits are especially important to you as he is your ruler. Jupiter is the planet of luck and opportunities and, since November of 2018, he has moved into your sign. This will make 2019 not only the year when you fully resurrect but will help you feel stronger and better than before. If Saturn cleared the slate 2015-2018, Jupiter is now painting a new identity for you. A new brand, a new body, new business cards, a new web site, a new self. 2019 is super exciting, and you will regain your enthusiasm and full-blown optimistic vibe that makes you so irresistible. It is a great year to change your clothes, your public image, to connect to a new physical activity or sport. You will see people starting to notice you more than before and appreciate what you have to offer.

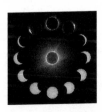

The 5 Eclipses –
Your Emotional Landscape

Eclipses quicken processes and push events towards completion. They are wild-cards, amplifiers of whatever is happening in your life. They also weave stories through an endless magical tapestry of synchronicities and dreams. The eclipses this year are shifting into Cancer and Capricorn and since the North Node is in Cancer it asks us to focus on our feelings, security, compassion, and family. The Nodes represent the junction between the paths of the sun and the moon, the conjunction of the father and mother's influence. The North Node, also dubbed the Head of the Dragon, represents what our soul desires. The South Node, which is in the opposite side of the zodiac, hence in Capricorn, represents what our soul desires to let go. That means we must shed the dark side of Capricorn: fear, ignorance, lack of tolerance, fixation to the status quo, conservatism, and nationalism. Fear is partly designed to ensure our survival but being over preoccupied with ourselves and our survival can hamper the ability to see and relate to others. That is where Cancer comes in and teaches us compassion and empathy.

The eclipses this year in January, July, and December will bring us opportunities to face our fears, confront the devil, and come out winning using the magic of compassion, unconditional love, and loving-kindness.

The eclipses, being in Cancer and Capricorn, are not that easy for you as you are a Fire-Bender and water and earth don't sit that well with you. For this reason, January, July, and December can be a bit more emotional and challenging. During the eclipses, you will feel an especially strong push and pull between home and career, feelings and responsibilities, mother and father, withdrawal and exposure. The eclipses can bring a great deal of fears and insecurities from early childhood.

In your specific case, the eclipses fall in your house of money, talents, and self-worth as well as the house of death, sexuality, and transformation. You already started feeling the effect of these eclipses in July 2018. The eclipses in 2019 will force you to shift some of the focus from your talents to the talents of other people. It is a good year to receive an inheritance and connect to other people's gifts and investments. The eclipses can also bring about powerful healing and therapy.

January 5–6: Partial Solar Eclipse in Capricorn. This New Moon in Capricorn falls in your house of money, talents, and self-worth. This is the time to start a new money-making venture. A new talent coming to the forefront and a new opportunity to be seen and noticed.

January 20–21: Total Lunar Eclipse Leo/Cancer cusp. This full moon takes place right on the border between Cancer and Leo and falls between your houses of transformation and travel. There could be a push and pull between your talent or money and your partner's, forcing you to make some compromises in order to work with other people. The eclipse also pits home and family opposite to career, mother versus father, your needs and your community's needs. This lunar eclipse can be especially emotional.

July 2, 2019: Total Solar Eclipse Cancer. This new moon marks a new beginning in your family life or emotional space. The key phrase here is "I feel!" Good time to start a family and make a move to a new location. The eclipse falls in your house of sexuality, passion, and transformation. It is a great time for healing sexual issues, to shed and transform, as well as embark on a study of the occult. It is a great opportunity to dive deep into your subconscious and retrieve hidden gifts.

July 16–17, 2019: Partial Lunar Eclipse Capricorn. This full moon in Capricorn again pits career versus home and family, mother figures versus father figures. You can see that this is a recurring theme of the year. The eclipse falls in your house of finance as well as your partner's income. You will have to let go of your ego in order to improve your financial situation, especially if you have a partner in work or life.

December 26, 2019: Annular Solar Eclipse Capricorn. This new moon in Capricorn falls in your house of money, joining Saturn, Pluto, as well as Jupiter. A great deal of action and new beginning even if it is the end of the year and holidays. The key phrase is "I Use." Try to use whatever resources you have to manifest new aspects in your career. This eclipse echoes the eclipse of Jan 5 and falls in your house of income and talent. A possibility for a raise or promotion or a new idea that can help you make more money or feel better about yourself.

 ## Mercury Retrograde – Mental Landscape

During Mercury retrograde, it is not recommended to start new long-term projects, sign documents, make large purchases, get married, publish, start marketing campaigns, or release new products. Communications of all sorts are slower and filled with glitches and challenges. Computers crash; stock markets turn volatile; flights are delayed; traffic is worse than usual; accidents occur more often; and Murphy's Law takes hold of our lives. For example, the infamous Flash Crash of May 6, 2010, took place during Mercury retrograde in Taurus (the sign of money and the stock market). If you need to fly during Mercury retro, make sure you do your online check-in and take longer to reach the airport. Try to avoid overscheduling yourself or being overly critical and demanding. Also pay attention to your diet and food intake.

If you must start a new project, be as mindful as you can. Pay attention to small details and read in-between the lines if you must sign a document. Rewrite your emails, edit your texts, and think before you speak. In fact, it is better if you spend more time listening than talking. Life does not come to a halt during Mercury retrograde. You can still achieve a great deal. Mercury retro is like going on a vacation while it is raining. It is still possible but not much fun. However, it is a great time to edit, redo, reexamine yourself and your path, revisit old projects, and find lost objects. It is said that there are more coincidences and synchronicities while Mercury is retrograding. Try to focus on activities that have the prefix re – reevaluate, reedit, redo, reexamine, reconnect, regenerate, revisit, re-imagine, etc.

This year Mercury is retrograding in water signs. Because you belong to the fire clan, it might be a bit more challenging as water and fire do not mix well. This combination can create steam, which translates to over thinking. As a Fire-Bender, you might experience emotional moments during the retrogrades.

Between March 5 and March 28, Mercury retrogrades in Pisces, which falls in your house of home and family. This can create misunderstanding and confusion with family members. You might have glitches or malfunctions at your home or office. Not a good time to buy property. During this retrograde, certain aspects of ancestral karma might surface. These could range from addiction to self-destructiveness, anger issues, etc.

Between July 7 and July 31, Mercury retrogrades in Leo and then moves to Cancer, shifting the confusion from your house of travel and education to the house of death and sexuality. Be extra careful with insurance and taxes as well as dealing with investments. There could also be some difficulties communicating with family members. You might find parenting to be harder than normal. Problems with lands and real-estate. Shame, guilt, passive-aggressiveness. Be careful with traveling abroad. Conflict can arise with in-laws. This retrograde is especially harsh as it falls during the eclipses of mid-July.

Between October 31 to November 20, Mercury retrogrades in Scorpio in your house of past lifetime, jails, hospitals, and confinement. Be extra careful with addictions and relapses. This is an especially challenging retrograde that can turn aggressive and deadly so take heed.

Unpredictability, Originality and a Touch of Chaos

In May 2018, Uranus moved into Taurus and will stay there until 2026, falling in your house of work, health, diet, and routine. From 2010 until 2018, Uranus was in your house of love and children, causing a great deal of chaos and movement with your creativity, romance and happiness and now, for the next 7 years, Uranus will bring disruption but also innovation into your work.

Uranus is called "the Joker" or "the Fool." It is chaotic but also ingenious. You might suddenly get an "aha" moment that can help your better understand your work as well as your health.

However, due to Uranus' retrograde motion, he reentered your house of love, children, and happiness in November 7, 2018 and will be there until March 6, 2019. This means that, for the first two months of the year, Uranus will be creating a bit more chaos with your love life, children, and creativity.

From March 6 until 2026, Uranus might inspire you to take a leap of faith into something totally new regarding your workspace or profession. Maybe a new field of work that can later translate into a new revenue stream. Since Uranus is disruptive, he can cause sudden changes in your diet or health. Try to be consistent.

Uranus favors technology, innovation, and science. Maybe you can think of a great new application or an e-commerce business. 2019 is a great year to integrate technology with your work or to update your professional life. Some employees or coworkers will act crazy and behave in an unpredictable way. Think outside of the box and your work with thrive.

Mars –
Energy and Passion

Mars governs vegetation, action, leadership, passion, and aggression. This year, Mars will not be traveling in your sign. But don't feel bad, he will be paying you a visit from January 2 of 2020. Below is a list of Mars' transits through the signs that can help you determine where to focus your energy. However, remember that even the best fighters need a general. Make sure you pace yourself and control your inner warrior.

 January 1 to Feb 14

You might feel aggressive but also powerful enough to manifest your wishes. This is a good time to exercise or find a new physical activity that can improve your health. Since Mars is now in your house of love, recreational activities, sports, hobbies, and fun, these aspects will blossom. Your inner child is active but be careful of injuries. If you have kids, they might create some conflicts and arguments.

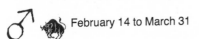 February 14 to March 31

This transit can help you boost your finances. It is a good time to invest in your talent and express your gifts as well as stand up for your values. Be careful not to overspend money. This aspect can give you extra energy and passion in your work, as well as help you find new ways to serve. A great time for diet and changes of routine. Be careful of arguments and fights with employees and coworkers. Be extra careful of injuries, inflammations, and stress. Since Uranus and Mars are coming together, be extra careful with injuries, accidents, and mishaps.

March 31 to May 16

It is a great time for winning arguments, getting help with legal affairs, and can also provide you with extra energy in business and writing. Be careful of fights with relatives, roommates, siblings, or neighbors. Mars is transiting in your house of relationships; therefore, it is great time for projects with partners. Be careful of lawsuits or conflict with enemies. This is a classic aspect of breakups. So be extra careful. It is also a time when you might embark on a crusade against your enemies.

 May 16 to July 1

Good time to renovate your home, office or workspace. This Mars location can cause unnecessary conflict with your family. This is a powerful transit for Mars. Your passion, sexuality, and intimacy are heightened. You will feel attractive and be able to attract opportunities in finance, investments, and production. Your own healing abilities can grow as well as the ability to help other people tap into their talents and finances. You can ride the dragon (North Node in Cancer) towards the underworld to retrieve hidden talents and passions.

 July 1 to August 18

A wonderful time for recreational activities, sports, hobbies, and fun. You might feel a need to engage in risky endeavors so take heed with implosive behaviors. Love is in the air as well as creativity. Your inner child is active but be careful of injuries. This transit of Mars falls in your house of travel and education. A great time for adventures and embarking on a journey to a place you have never visited either physically (traveling) or mentally (through study). It is a time to fight for your truth. Some conflict can take place with in-laws.

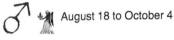 August 18 to October 4

This time can provide extra energy and passion in your work as well as help you find a new way to serve. A great time for diet and changes of routine. Once again, be aware of strife with employees and coworkers. This transit of Mars takes place in your house of career. It is a good time to assert yourself and ask for a promotion or assume a leadership role. Be careful of conflicts with bosses, father figures, or competitive colleagues.

 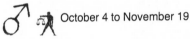 October 4 to November 19

A great time for projects with partners. Be careful of lawsuits or conflict with enemies. You might find yourself needing to spend more time or energy with partners. Mars falls in your house of community, friends, companies, and clubs. You will feel extra competitive with people in your group of friends or company. It is a good time for team sports or any activity that involves a community. Be careful of fights or politics in your company.

November 19 to January 2, 2020

This is a powerful transit for Mars. Your passion, sexuality, and interest in intimacy is heightened. You will feel attractive and be able to attract opportunities in finance, investments, and production. Your own healing abilities can grow as well as the ability to help other people tap into their talents and finances. This transit takes place in your house of letting go, past lifetimes, hidden enemies, hospitals, jails, and confinement. Be extra careful of injuries or accidents that can lead to a visit to the ER. You also must be aware that you might make hidden enemies. Memories from past lives might return as well as meetings with people you have known in past lives.

Venus: Money and Love

Venus is the ruler of pleasure, luxury, finance, talents, values, art, and relationships. She is also associated with Maat, the goddess of justice and law. Venus works in beauty cycles: the more you love yourself, the more you believe in yourself. The better your self-image, the more you connect to your talents. The more you develop and invest in your talents, the more money you can make. Venus' message is: love yourself and money will follow.

This year, the goddess of beauty will be in your sign twice! From January 7 to Feb 3 and November 1 to November 26, Venus is making you more attractive, helping you get a raise, or tap into a new talent. These are great times for romance, making money, and connecting to your artistic side. These are also good times for you to re-brand yourself, dress differently, change your hair, or get some new clothes. Not a bad time to indulge and pamper yourself (if it is healthy and does not harm you or anyone else).

Conclusion:

2019 is a great year. With Jupiter, your planet, coming to bless your tribe for the first 11 months of 2019, you will feel that opportunities come your way and that doors slide open effortlessly. The place you need to focus this year is rebuilding your self-worth, tapping and investing in your talents, and changing the way you make money so that your values are congruent with your finances. This is also a year to heal, connect to your passion and sexuality, and let go of whatever is already dead in your life.

22ND DECEMBER – 19TH JANUARY

CAPRICORN

Sometimes I wonder who am I? The world seeming to pass me by.*

key phrase
I USE

element
Cardinal earth

planet
Saturn, the lord of karma and understanding

day
Saturday

incentive
Business plan

body parts
Skin, teeth, skeleton, knees

color
Indigo

stone
Garnet, black onyx, hematite

---

* Lou Reed, 2003.

I USE WHAT I HAVE TO SHARE.

 2019 Integration:
Me and you

What a year 2018 has been for your tribe! And what a year you are about to begin. To be honest, the journey is just beginning. 2020 is the year where everyone around you will try to be you, since we will have a convergence of planets in your sign. I know you are good with long-term projects, running long distances, and being patient, but life has been challenging for you since Saturn moved into your sign in the end of 2017. Usually having Saturn in your sign is not easy, but for you, hosting the planet of karma is not a big deal. After all, Saturn is your ruler and has a special relationship with you. The last time Saturn was in your sign was 1989-1991. You can return to that period to see how Saturn worked with you and what your lessons were back then. These lessons are bound to return and continue your karmic education for the next two years.

From December 2017 to end of 2020, Saturn, the grand teacher and rectifier, is transiting in your house of body, personality, and identity. 2019 and 2020 are crucial in defining your next three decades. You are now sculpting a new identity, a new body, a new temperament. In these years, you can transcend your genetics, conditioning, and childhood traumas or patterns. You have the power through discipline, persistence, and endurance to change not only your physical body but also your character and nature. You can rebrand yourself, embarking on a new path that can change everything from your finances to your relationships, where you live and who your friends are. It is a rare opportunity to be someone new, especially as it is happening in the year you are supposed to give birth to your inner child.

2019 might feel like Saturn is reconstructing you by first causing you to erase your old self. Saturn is not an easy planet and you might have to deal with injuries, physical pain, and setbacks before you can rebuild your new personality. I recommend starting a new exercise regimen, changing your clothes and style, changing your hair, maybe even changing cities or neighborhoods. I know change is not easy for you but in December, Jupiter, the planet of luck, is moving for the first time in 12 years into your sign. This is great news as in 2020 you will have Jupiter helping you experience a great deal of opportunities and expansion. In fact, the Tarot card "two of disks" is associated with Jupiter in Capricorn and is called "Change." Change is coming, and this year you can decide the course and direction of this change.

2019 is especially intense since you not only have Saturn in your sign, but also Pluto, the lord of death and transformation, as well as the South Node. Pluto has been in your sign since 2008. So that is not news, but the South Node has not been in your sign since 2000 and 2001, and that demands some attention. Having the South Node in your sign means that the next two years the eclipses will fall in Capricorn and/or opposite to you, in Cancer. The eclipse of January 5 as well as that of December 26 are Solar Eclipses in Capricorn, which means you will have the Sun and the Moon conjunct very close to your birthday. Whenever the eclipses fall on or close to your birthday, the year is considered full of events and transformation.

When the South Node falls in your sign and in your first house it means that you have to let go of the dark side of your sign: ignorance, fear, greed, over attachment to the stats-quo, and the fear of change. But you also have to let go of yourself, of your ego, of the fear of survival. And here is where the paradox of 2019 also manifests for you. I just told you that you need to focus on changing *yourself* and yet the South Node asks you not to focus on yourself but on *others*. On one hand, you have the cluster of planets in your house of I-me-mine, trying to teach you about who you are and help you rebuild a new you. On the other hand, you have the North Node in the house of relationships, telling you that you must let go of you and focus on your partner and significant other. Maybe the integration is that you must let go of who you were, detach yourself from aspects of your ego that hold you back, so a new you can come out of the ashes effortlessly and be available for a real partnership.

When the South Node is in the house of "me," it means that the North Node is in the house of "us." This year you need to focus on learning the lessons of your opposite sign, Cancer, as well as on the house of relationships and partners. You must embody the teaching of compassion, unconditional love, and forgiveness, especially in the context of relationships. Put together, this year you are being scrutinized and trained by Saturn. You are asked to rebuild and reevaluate your identity as well as carve a new path for yourself in life. That should be done by focusing on creating, attracting, and maintaining partnerships in work and in life, as well as by letting go of fear. Sounds like too much? Not for you. Especially when Jupiter moves to your sign in December to give you the godsent boon you need to move mountains.

Jupiter this year is traveling through your house of mysticism, past lifetimes, and letting go. It is a great time to start yoga, meditate, dance, martial arts, or to reconnect to abilities and gifts you might have had in a past lifetime. There might be a new location or talent or people who would come into your life and feel familiar.

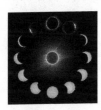

The 5 Eclipses – Your Emotional Landscape

Eclipses quicken processes and push events towards completion. They are wild-cards, amplifiers of whatever is happening in your life. They also weave stories through an endless magical tapestry of synchronicities and dreams. The eclipses this year, as I just stated before, are shifting into Cancer and your sign. Since the North Node is in Cancer, it asks us to focus on our feelings, security, compassion, and family. The North Node represents the junction between the paths of the sun and the moon, the conjunction of the father and mother's influence. The North Node, also dubbed the Head of the Dragon, represents what our soul desires. The South Node, which is in the opposite side of the zodiac, hence in Capricorn, represents what our soul desires to let go. That means we must shed the dark side of Capricorn: fear, ignorance, lack of tolerance, fixation to the status quo, conservatism, and nationalism. Fear is partly designed to ensure our survival but being over preoccupied with you and your survival can hamper your ability to see and relate to others. That is where Cancer comes in and teaches us compassion and empathy. The ability to walk in other people's shoes. The eclipses this year in January, July, and December will bring us opportunities to face our fears, confront the devil, and come out winning using the magic of compassion and unconditional love.

During the eclipses you will feel an especially strong push and pull between home and career, feelings and responsibilities, mother and father, withdrawal and exposure. The eclipses can bring a great deal of fears and insecurities from early childhood. Since the eclipses occur in your sign and your opposite sign, they will also make you feel pushed and pulled between your needs and your partner's needs. It will be a time of "I" versus "thou." Balance and compromises are your best way to deal with the eclipses.

January 5–6: Partial Solar Eclipse in your sign. This New Moon in Capricorn falls in your first house of body and personality. A new side of your character may be revealed. It is a good time to get new business cards, a new web site, or to launch something new in your life.

January 20–21: Total Lunar Eclipse Leo/Cancer cusp. This full moon takes place right on the border between Cancer and Leo and falls between your houses of relationships and sexuality. This eclipse puts home and family opposite to career, mother versus father, your needs and your community's needs. It can also activate fears of death and intimacy. This lunar eclipse can be especially emotional.

July 2, 2019: Total Solar Eclipse Cancer. This new moon marks a new beginning in your family life or emotional space. The key word here is "I feel!" Good time to start a family and make a move to a new location. This new moon falls in your house of relationships. A new partnership or a new connection with someone that can become very important in your life.

July 16–17, 2019: Partial Lunar Eclipse Capricorn. This full moon in Capricorn again pits career versus home and family, mother figures versus father figures. You can see that this is a recurring theme of the year. It will also create an opposition between you and your partner in work or in life. Be extra careful in lawsuits and with enemies.

December 26, 2019: Annular Solar Eclipse Capricorn. This new moon in Capricorn falls in your house of body, personality, and image. A great deal of action and new beginning even if it is the end of the year and holidays. The key phrase is "I Use." Try to use whatever resources you have to manifest new aspects in your career and create a new identity.

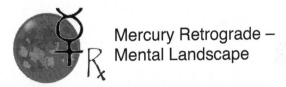

Mercury Retrograde – Mental Landscape

During Mercury retrograde, it is not recommended to start new long-term projects, sign documents, make large purchases, get married, publish, start marketing campaigns, or release new products. Communications of all sorts are slower and filled with glitches and challenges. Computers crash; stock markets turn volatile; flights are delayed; traffic is worse than usual; accidents occur more often; and Murphy's Law takes hold of our lives. For example, the infamous Flash Crash of May 6, 2010, took place during Mercury retrograde in Taurus (the sign of money and the stock market). If you need to fly during Mercury retro, make sure you do your online check-in and take longer to reach the airport. Try to avoid overscheduling yourself or being overly critical and demanding. Also pay attention to your diet and food intake.

If you must start a new project, be as mindful as you can. Pay attention to small details and read in-between the lines if you must sign a document. Rewrite your emails, edit your texts, and think before you speak. In fact, it is better if you spend more time listening than talking. Life does not come to a halt during Mercury retrograde. You can still achieve a great deal. Mercury retro is like going on a vacation while it is raining. It is still possible but not much fun. However, it is a great time to edit, redo, reexamine yourself and your path, revisit old projects, and find lost objects. It is said that there are more coincidences and synchronicities while Mercury is retrograding. Try to focus on activities that have the prefix re – reevaluate, reedit, redo, reexamine, reconnect, regenerate, revisit, re-imagine, etc.

This year, Mercury is retrograding in water signs. Because you belong to the earth clan, the retrogrades might be a bit easier than usual. As an Earth-Bender, you might experience some irregularities with your schedule and work and some emotional moments during the retrogrades.

Between March 5 and March 28, Mercury retrogrades in Pisces, which falls in your house of communication. This means that all forms of communication will experience delay or misunderstanding. You should be extra careful with contracts and communication with siblings and relatives.

Between July 7 and July 31, Mercury retrogrades in Leo and then moves to Cancer shifting the confusion from your house of death and transformation to the house of relationships. There could be miscommunication between you and those with whom you experience intimacy and close relationships. Be especially be careful of enemies or lawsuits. This retrograde is especially hard as it takes place at the same time of the eclipse.

Between October 31 and November 20, Mercury retrogrades in Scorpio in your house of community, people, and government. Be extra vigilant with taxes, permits, and bureaucracy. There might be miscommunication with friends or coworkers in your company or corporation.

 Unpredictability, Originality and a Touch of Chaos

In May 2018, Uranus moved into Taurus and will stay there until 2026, falling in your house of children, love, and creativity. Uranus is the rebel and is often called "the Joker" or "the Fool." He is chaotic but also ingenious. You might suddenly get an "aha" moment that can help you deal better with your children or with your lover or with creative projects. Uranus can also cause you to suddenly fall in and out of love or feel as if you are on a roller coaster with your happiness level or moods. There might be some rebellious tendencies with your kids and if they are teenagers, well, your unconditional love will be tested.

However, due to Uranus' retrograde motion, he reentered your house of home and family in November 7, 2018 and will be there until March 6, 2019. This means that for the first two months of the year, Uranus will be creating a bit more chaos with your family.

From March 6, Uranus might inspire you to take a leap of faith into a new creative field or a new sport or hobby. This can help you with the creation of a new identity we discussed earlier. Since Uranus favors innovation and technology, try to implement these things in your creation and recreational activities.

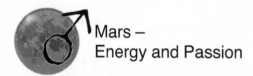

Mars – Energy and Passion

This year, Mars is not transiting in your sign, but you will still be guided by his fierce energy as he transits in your different houses. Below is a list of Mars' transits through the signs that can help you determine where to focus your energy. However, remember that even the best fighters need a general. Make sure you pace yourself and control your inner warrior.

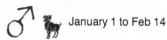 January 1 to Feb 14

You might feel aggressive but also powerful enough to manifest your wishes. This is a good time to exercise or find a new physical activity that can improve your health. Good time to renovate your home, office, or workspace. This Mars location can cause unnecessary conflict with your family. Be extra careful of passive-aggressiveness or making others feel guilty. Actions and feelings need to connect.

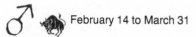 February 14 to March 31

This transit can help you boost your finances. It is a good time to invest in your talent and express your gifts as well as stand up for your values. Be careful not to overspend money. Recreational activities, sports, hobbies, and fun. Love is in the air as well as creativity. Your

166

inner child is active but be careful of injuries. If you have kids, they might create some conflicts and arguments. Uranus and Mars are coming together so be careful of accidents and mishaps.

  March 31 to May 16

It is a great time for winning arguments, getting help with legal affairs, and can also provide you with extra energy in business and writing. This aspect can give you extra energy and passion in your work, as well as helping you find a new way to serve. A great time for diet and changes of routine. Be careful of arguments and fights with employees and coworkers. Be extra careful of injuries, inflammations, and stress.

 May 16 to July 1

Good time to renovate your home, office, or workspace. This Mars location can cause unnecessary conflict with your family. Mars is transiting in your house of relationships; therefore, it is great time for projects with partners. Be careful of lawsuits or conflict with enemies. This is a classic aspect of breakups. So be extra careful. It is also a time when you might embark on a crusade against your enemies. With the North Node in Cancer, you can ride your dragon towards healing and attracting your relationships.

  July 1 to August 18

A wonderful time for recreational activities, sports, hobbies, and fun. You might feel a need to engage in risky endeavors so take heed with implosive behaviors. Love is in the air as well as creativity. This is a powerful transit for Mars. Your passion, sexuality, and intimacy are heightened. You will feel attractive and be able to attract opportunities in finance, investments, and production. Your own healing abilities can grow as well as the ability to help other people tap into their talents and finance.

 August 18 to October 4

This time can provide extra energy and passion in your work and maybe entice you to find a mission or a new way to serve. Another good time for diet and changes of routine. Be extra patient with employees and coworkers. This transit of Mars falls in your house of travel and education. A great time for adventures and embarking on a journey to a place you have never visited either physically (traveling) or mentally (through study). It is a time to fight for your truth. Some conflict can take place with in-laws.

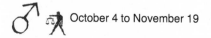 October 4 to November 19

A great time for action and movement with partners in life and work. Some fights might take place with partners. This transit of Mars takes place in your house of career. It is a good time to assert yourself and ask for a promotion or assume a leadership role. Be careful of conflicts with bosses, father figures, or competitive colleagues.

 November 19 to January 2, 2020

This is a powerful transit for Mars. Your passion, sexuality, and interest in intimacy is heightened. You will feel attractive and be able to attract opportunities. Mars falls in your house of community, friends, companies, and clubs. You will feel extra competitive with people in your group of friends or company. It is a good time for team sports or any activity that involves a community. Be careful of fights or politics in your company.

Venus: Money and Love

Venus is the ruler of pleasure, luxury, finance, talents, values, art, and relationships. She is also associated with Maat, the goddess of justice and law. Venus works in beauty cycles: the more you love yourself, the more you believe in yourself. The better your self-image, the more you connect to your talents. The more you develop and invest in your talents, the more money you can make. Venus' message is: love yourself and money will follow.

This year, the goddess of beauty will be in your sign twice! Between February 3 and March 1 as well as between November 26 and December 20, Venus is making you more attractive, helping you get a raise, or tap into a new talent. It is a great time for romance, making money, and connecting to your artistic side. This is a good time for you to rebrand yourself, dress differently, change your hair, or get some new clothes. Not a bad time to indulge and pamper yourself (if it is healthy and does not harm you or anyone else).

Conclusion:

This year you are going through a big shift in all aspects of your life. Brace yourself for change and allow the universe to flow through you. This year is a rare combination sof planetary influences and eclipses that can help you morph your life in a new desirable way. Make sure you use Jupiter's journey in the house of mysticism to connect to meditation and let go of things that hold you back. Also, this is a year to focus on partnership in work or in life.

21ST JANUARY – 18TH FEBRUARY

AQUARIUS

Let it go, let it go, can't hold it back anymore. *

key phrase
I KNOW

element
Fixed (unchangeable) air

planet
Uranus

day
Saturday

incentive
Friendship

body parts
Ankles, shinbones and circulatory system

color
Violet

stone
Sapphire

---

* Frozen, 2013.

170

I KNOW EMPATHY.

 ## 2019 Integration: Serve others while serving myself

2019 continues your journey in the mysterious house of mysticism, past lifetimes, empathy, poetry, dance, hospitalization, confinement, and letting go. I must be honest, there is no sugar coating this placement for Saturn. He is deep in what is called the "house of suffering," but it is also dubbed the "house of enlightenment." If you stop to think about it, and thinking is something your tribe of Aquarius is known for, everyone who attained enlightenment did so after a long period of suffering. The Buddha and Christ had three temptations and a visitation from the devil himself before they received their illumination. You too are now walking in the shadow of death, and you should fear no evil. It has been going on for the last year-and-a-half and it will continue until 2021 when Saturn moves into your sign.

Saturn's journey in your house of letting go is not bad. It is a powerful opportunity once in 30 years to shed everything about your life or your personality that holds you back. It is a time when you can strip naked and expose your weaknesses so they can be vanquished. It is a time to surrender, to become like water, and flow with life instead of trying to control it. With this transit of Saturn, you might experience a great deal of memories from past lifetimes. Maybe you will find yourself excelling in new skills that you had prior experience with. It could be that you find yourself in a new city or country that feels familiar or a new person walking into your life with whom you develop instant intimacy as if you knew each other for years.

Saturn's transit in this house (called the 12th house which is the number of this year) can make you feel more vulnerable and sensitive.

As you open to your spiritual side and experience empathy and intuition, psychic hits, prophetic dreams, and visions, you might also feel depressed or sad at times. It is as if you pick up other people's energies and absorb their pain. You might feel lethargic or with no energy to achieve your goals. It makes sense. Don't be critical with yourself. It is a good time to try to sleep more, but also swimming, walking by a water source, and meditating can elevate the negative feelings.

This year's paradox for your tribe is to integrate the need to serve others and engage in your work (your North Node is in the house of work), while learning how to retreat from life and serve yourself. You need to balance your space with other people's space. On one hand, be there for everyone but also carve place for yourself and your time alone. Not easy for an Aquarius, the sign of altruism that is so afraid of being called selfish.

Jupiter always comes to the rescue and this year it is transiting in the house of friends, community, and hope. That's great news to you water-bearers because you are the sign of fraternity, altruism, community, and hope. Right in your winter of discontent, Jupiter is coming with the cavalry. Jupiter is now in your house of manifesting wishes and, since Saturn is in your house of mysticism, the combination can make your prayers come true and your dreams manifest. Jupiter in your house of friends can also mean that help will come from friends, spending time with people, and joining new organizations. If you are working in a company or in a corporation, there might be a raise or promotion as well as an offer from a new company. Maybe a new friend is coming into your life, someone you knew in a previous life.

Uranus, the ruler of your chart is moving a sign, from Aries to Taurus, and it always affects you when Uranus makes a move. You will feel the chaotic energies of your ruler in the house of home and family. It already started May 2018 but will become more dominant from

March 2019. This could mean a sudden change of residence, relocation, unexpected disruption with family members, and maybe moving to a home in a place that feels more like a community.

Since the North Node moved into Cancer, it means the eclipses are shifting towards the house of service. One of the remedies to the pain and suffering afflicted by Saturn is focusing on service to others. This year, place extra focus on your diet, health, routine, and work.

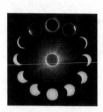

The 5 Eclipses –
Your Emotional Landscape

Eclipses quicken processes and push events towards completion. They are wild-cards, amplifiers of whatever is happening in your life. They also weave stories through an endless magical tapestry of synchronicities and dreams. The eclipses this year are shifting into Cancer and Capricorn and since the North Node is in Cancer it asks us to focus on our feelings, security, compassion, and family. The Nodes represent the junction between the paths of the sun and the moon, the conjunction of the father and mother's influence. The North Node, also dubbed the Head of the Dragon, represents what our soul desires. The South Node, which is in the opposite side of the zodiac, hence in Capricorn, represents what our soul desires to let go. That means we must shed the dark side of Capricorn: fear, ignorance, lack of tolerance, fixation to the status quo, conservatism, and nationalism. Fear is partly designed to ensure our survival but being over preoccupied with ourselves and our survival can hamper the ability to see and relate to others. That is where Cancer comes in and teaches us compassion and empathy.

The eclipses this year in January, July, and December will bring us opportunities to face our fears, confront the devil, and come out winning using the magic of compassion, unconditional love, and loving-kindness.

In 2017 and 2018, the eclipses fell in your sign and, especially in February and August of these years, you felt life moving faster. This is over and the eclipses this year fall in the houses of letting go and the house of work and service. The North Node, as we saw, is what you need to focus on this year. The lessons for you this year are the teachings of compassion and empathy. Where should you focus this compassion? In your case, in the house of work and service. This is a year where you have to let go of your own suffering and focus on serving others. January, July, and December are the time these lessons would be strongest. In addition, during the eclipses, you will feel an especially strong push and pull between home and career, feelings and responsibilities, mother and father, withdrawal and exposure. The eclipses can bring a great deal of fears and insecurities from early childhood.

January 5–6: Partial Solar Eclipse in Capricorn. This New Moon in Capricorn falls in your house of letting go, mysticism, and past lives. By initiating a process of letting go, your career can present new opportunities. The best time in the year to start a meditation routine.

January 20–21: Total Lunar Eclipse Leo/Cancer cusp. This full moon takes place right on the border between Cancer and Leo and falls between your houses of work and relationships. Lunar eclipses represent oppositions. In this case, it is pitting home and family opposite to career, mother versus father, your needs and your community's needs. This lunar eclipse can be especially emotional. You will also experience a push and pull between your needs and your partner's needs as well as the need to serve yourself versus the need to serve others.

July 2, 2019: Total Solar Eclipse Cancer. This new moon marks a new beginning in your family life or emotional space. The key phrase here is "I feel!" Good time to start a family and make a move to a new location. The eclipse falls in your house of work and service. This is a good time to start something new in your work, a new diet, or a new focus on healing and your body.

July 16–17, 2019: Partial Lunar Eclipse Capricorn. This full moon in Capricorn again pits career versus home and family, mother figures versus father figures. You can see that this is a recurring theme of the year. Once again, you will be asked to let go of something in your life in order for your health and or work to improve.

December 26, 2019: Annular Solar Eclipse Capricorn. This new moon in Capricorn falls in your house of mystical experiences and letting go joining Saturn, Pluto, as well as Jupiter. A great deal of action and new beginning even if it is the end of the year and holidays. The key phrase is "I Use." Try to use whatever resources you have to manifest new aspects in your career. The eclipse falls in your house of mystical experiences, dreams, and letting go. You can see that the theme of cutting things that hold you back out of your life, is recurring.

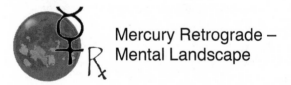

Mercury Retrograde – Mental Landscape

During Mercury retrograde, it is not recommended to start new long-term projects, sign documents, make large purchases, get married, publish, start marketing campaigns, or release new products. Communications of all sorts are slower and filled with glitches and challenges. Computers crash; stock markets turn volatile; flights are delayed; traffic is worse than usual; accidents occur more often; and Murphy's Law takes hold of our lives. For example, the infamous Flash Crash of May 6, 2010, took place during Mercury retrograde in Taurus (the sign of money and the stock market). If you need to fly during Mercury retro, make sure you do your online check-in and take longer to reach the airport. Try to avoid overscheduling yourself or being overly critical and demanding. Also pay attention to your diet and food intake.

If you must start a new project, be as mindful as you can. Pay attention to small details and read in-between the lines if you must sign a document. Rewrite your emails, edit your texts, and think before you speak. In fact, it is better if you spend more time listening than talking. Life does not come to a halt during Mercury retrograde. You can still achieve a great deal. Mercury retro is like going on a vacation while it is raining. It is still possible but not much fun. However, it is a great time to edit, redo, reexamine yourself and your path, revisit old projects, and find lost objects. It is said that there are more coincidences and synchronicities while Mercury is retrograding. Try to focus on activities that have the prefix *re* – reevaluate, reedit, redo, reexamine, reconnect, regenerate, revisit, re-imagine, etc.

This year, Mercury is retrograding in water signs. Because you belong to the air clan, it might be a bit more challenging as water and air do not mix well. As an Air-Bender, you might experience emotional bubbles or fantasies that can burst in your face. Watch what you say and write very carefully this year.

Between March 5 and March 28, Mercury retrogrades in Pisces, which falls in your house of money, talents, and self-worth. Be extra careful with finances and spending. Avoid big purchases. Your self-worth might be shaken by mistakes or certain mishaps.

Between July 7 and July 31, Mercury retrogrades in Leo and then moves to Cancer, shifting the confusion from your house of relationships to the house of work. This can cause misunderstanding and miscommunication with partners in life and work as well as family members. Be careful with relationships with employees and coworkers and watch your diet.

Between October 31 and November 20, Mercury retrogrades in Scorpio in your house of career. This can cause miscommunication, delays, and frustrations in your professional life and especially with bosses and father figures. Watch your relationship with your father or anyone you consider a mentor.

 Unpredictability, Originality and a Touch of Chaos

In May 2018, Uranus, your ruler, moved into Taurus and will stay there until 2026, falling in your house of home and family. This means that from 2018, your home life, sense of security, real-estate, as well as your family of origin are going through a rollercoaster with a great deal of unpredictable twists and changes. This happens every 84 years and Uranus will be transiting in that house until 2026. Since Uranus is your planet, you can channel his quirky energy easier than others.

Uranus is called "the Joker" or "the Fool." It is chaotic but also ingenious. You might suddenly get an "aha" moment that can help your dealing in real-estate as well as relationships with family members. Uranus can also bring humor and excitement to the home front and maybe even make you move to a place that has a strong sense of community. If you are planning a move, make sure your new home is innovative and connected to new technologies.

However, due to Uranus' retrograde motion, he reentered your house of communication and contracts from November 7, 2018 and will be there until March 6, 2019. This means that for the first two months of the year Uranus will be creating a bit more chaos with some contracts, your communications, and maybe relationships with your relatives.

Uranus favors technology, innovation, and science. Maybe you can think of how you can upgrade your home, maybe make it greener or add solar panels. It is a good time to start inviting friends to your home and making your residence a gathering place for lectures or potlucks.

Mars –
Energy and Passion

Mars governs vegetation, action, leadership, passion, and aggression. This year, Mars will not be transiting in your sign. However, you will still be influenced by his transits in your houses.

Below is a list of Mars' transits through the signs that can help you determine where to focus your energy. However, remember that even the best fighters need a general. Make sure you pace yourself and control your inner warrior.

 January 1 to Feb 14

You might feel aggressive but also powerful enough to manifest your wishes. This is a good time to exercise or find a new physical activity that can improve your health. Mars transiting in your house of communication is very good for business, getting contracts signed, closing deals, and can give you a boost in your writing. Be careful of fights with relatives, siblings, roommates, or neighbors. Your communication can cause conflict but also move mountains. Good for sales and marketing.

  February 14 to March 31

This transit can help you boost your finances. It is a good time to invest in your talents and express your gifts as well as stand up for your values. Be careful not to spend money. Mars in your house of home is good for renovation in your home, office, or workspace. This Mars location can cause unnecessary conflict with your family. Be extra careful of passive-aggressiveness or making others feel guilty. Actions and feelings need to connect. Uranus and Mars are coming together. So be careful of accidents and mishaps.

 March 31 to May 16

Extra energy in business, writing, marketing, and promotions. Be careful of fights with relatives, roommates, siblings, or neighbors. This transit can bring love into your life, connect you to your creativity, and is great for sports and fun. However, there could be conflict with your children and some fights with loved ones.

 May 16 to July 1

This Mars location can cause conflict with your family or people you live with. This aspect can give you extra energy and passion in your work, as well as help you find a new way to serve. A great time for diet and changes of routine. Be careful of arguments and fights with employees and coworkers. Be extra careful of injuries, inflammations, and stress. Since the North Node is in Cancer, you can ride the dragon towards your Promised Land in your work and health.

 July 1 to August 18

A wonderful time for recreational activities, sports, hobbies, and fun. You might feel a need to engage in risky endeavors so take heed with implosive behaviors. Love is in the air as well as creativity. Your inner child is active but be careful of injuries. Mars is transiting in your house of relationships. It is great time for projects with partners. Be careful of lawsuits or conflict with enemies. This is a classic aspect of breakups. So be extra careful. It is also a time when you might embark on a crusade against your enemies.

 August 18 to October 4

Mars is asking you to focus on your work and health. Mars can provide a project in work that demands more energy but also more passion. Be careful of arguments and fights with employees and coworkers as you might be extra pushy. This is a powerful transit for Mars. Your passion, sexuality, and intimacy are heightened. You will feel attractive and be able to attract opportunities in finance, investments, and production. Your own healing abilities can grow as well as the ability to help other people tap into their talents and finance.

October 4 to November 19

A great time for projects with partners. Be careful of lawsuits or conflict with enemies. Your partners in work or love might initiate fights or call you to action. This transit of Mars falls in your house of travel and education. A great time for adventures and embarking on a journey to a place you have never visited either physically (traveling) or mentally (through study). It is a time to fight for your truth. Some conflict can take place with in-laws.

 November 19 to January 2, 2020

This is a powerful transit for Mars. Your passion and intimacy are growing. You will find you are able to shed your old skin. This transit of Mars takes place in your house of career. It is a good time to assert yourself and ask for a promotion or assume a leadership role. Be careful of conflicts with bosses, father figures, or competitive colleagues.

 # Venus: Money and Love

Venus is the ruler of pleasure, luxury, finance, talents, values, art, and relationships. She is also associated with Maat, the goddess of justice and law. Venus works in beauty cycles: the more you love yourself, the more you believe in yourself. The better your self-image, the more you connect to your talents. The more you develop and invest in your talents, the more money you can make. Venus' message is: love yourself and money will follow.

This year, the goddess of beauty will be in your sign twice! She will be in your sign between March 1 and 26, as well as the last 10 days of 2019. In these times, Venus is making you more attractive, helping you get a raise, or tap into a new talent. These are great times for romance, making money, and connecting to your artistic side. These are also good times for you to rebrand yourself, dress differently, change your hair, or get some new clothes. Not a bad time to indulge and pamper yourself (if it is healthy and does not harm you or anyone else).

Conclusion:

2019 is the year when you have a rare opportunity connect to your mystical powers, empathy and healing, as well as remove obstacles from your life. If you ever wanted to go on a diet, let go of habits, addictions, or patterns, this year will be your year. In addition, this year offers a possibility to make new friends, connect to a new organization, and manifest your wishes. Remember, you serve others to also serve yourself!

19TH FEBRUARY – 20TH MARCH

PISCES

I get high with a little help from my friends.*

key phrase
I IMAGINE

element
Mutable (changeable) water

planet
Neptune, the lord of the oceans

day
Thursday

incentive
Mysticism

body parts
Feet, immune system, lymphatic system

color
Violet-black

stone
Amethyst

---

* The Beatles, 1967.

I IMAGINE
MY PERFECT COMMUNITY.

2019 Integration:
Mine versus other people's love and creativity

Pisces is a mute sign. Like the mermaids and mermen, they would rather chant, dance, swim, meditate, dream, and sleep than speak. But 2019 continues your journey in the house of community, fraternity, humanity, and hope, which means that you can do anything you like doing as long as you do it in a group or with your friends. This is a year to socialize, increase your amount of connections, work with NGOs and nonprofits, and allow humanity to enjoy the gifts you were given in this life.

Saturn, the Lord Karma, the grand teacher and rectifier, is helping you change your tribe and community. You will have to bid farewell to old companies, corporations, friends, and collogues and welcome new people and acquaintances. You have changed a great deal and now your friends will have to reflect that change. If you are working in a corporation or a company, there might be some change in management or how the organization runs. This will force change in your status in the organization. 2019 offers you a powerful opportunity to change your contact list, get rid of people that drain you, and bring new blood into your friendships.

In 2019, try to join new clubs and groups. Look for connectors that can help you create a new network. It is not an easy thing for you as you usually like solitude, but 2019 is a year to be in the center of your groups.

This year, Saturn is transiting in your house of wishes, manifestations, and hope. Not only can you make your wishes come true, you can also help others do the same. It is a year when people will ask you to use your psychic powers and intuition to help people around you. You can become an antenna of positivity, broadcasting hope. Since Saturn is in your house of government, make sure you have no issues with taxes or permits as some difficulties with bureaucracy can arise.

The paradox this year is between the need to focus on your love, happiness, children, and creativity (where you have the North Node) but still place a great deal of energy with your friends as well as other people's happiness and creativity. Should you focus on your love and children or should you spend time with a friend who is in need? Should you focus on your love or stay longer at work out of duty to your company? Remember, while it is true that you are a double sign and can multitask, it is important this year to focus on integration.

Jupiter is transiting in your house of career and that is great news for your professional life. Jupiter brings expansion, opportunity, and doors that open for you to make a leap in your career. This happens once in 12 years and, for this reason, you should roll up your sleeves and get down to business. With Saturn in your house of companies and Jupiter in the house of career, you might have to change company in order to manifest your true career potential. But regardless, Jupiter can create synchronicities to quicken your success in career as well as flow with bosses and authority figures. Maybe a new mentor or father figure is coming into your life.

The North Node moved into Cancer, a fellow water sign. This is great for you as you can easily swim with the aspect. The North Node is trying to teach us all empathy and compassion, traits that you already possess but must reclaim. The North Node is asking you to focus on love and happiness, connect to your children, creativity, and happiness. It is asking you to be more fun and entertaining in order to be successful in navigating this year. If you ever wanted to have a child or start your own "baby" project, 2019 and 2020 will be great for that.

The 5 Eclipses –
Your Emotional Landscape

Eclipses quicken processes and push events towards completion. They are wild-cards, amplifiers of whatever is happening in your life. They also weave stories through an endless magical tapestry of synchronicities and dreams. The eclipses this year are shifting into Cancer and Capricorn and since the North Node is in Cancer it asks us to focus on our feelings, security, compassion, and family. The Nodes represent the junction between the paths of the sun and the moon, the conjunction of the father and mother's influence. The North Node, also dubbed the Head of the Dragon, represents what our soul desires. The South Node, that is in the opposite side of the zodiac, hence in Capricorn, represents what our soul desires to let go. That means we must shed the dark side of Capricorn: fear, ignorance, lack of tolerance, fixation to the status quo, conservatism, and nationalism. Fear is partly designed to ensure our survival but being over preoccupied with ourselves and our survival can hamper the ability to see and relate to others. That is where Cancer comes in and teaches us compassion and empathy.

The eclipses this year in January, July, and December will bring us opportunities to face our fears, confront the devil, and come out winning using the magic of compassion, unconditional love, and loving-kindness.

The eclipses being in Cancer and Capricorn, are far easier for you than the eclipses in 2017 and 2018. During the eclipses, you will feel an especially strong push and pull between home and career, feelings and responsibilities, mother and father, withdrawal and exposure. The eclipses can bring a great deal of fears and insecurities from early childhood. In your case, the eclipses are asking you to let go of some of your friends, companies, and people around you and focus more on children, love, and your happiness.

January 5–6: Partial Solar Eclipse in Capricorn. This New Moon in Capricorn falls in your house of community and organizations. This could mean that a new friend is walking into your life who will be very significant or a new company. If you are happy with your organization, there could be some promotion or a new job description.

January 20–21: Total Lunar Eclipse Leo/Cancer cusp. This full moon takes place right on the border between Cancer and Leo and falls between your house of love and children and your house of health and work. Lunar eclipses represent oppositions. In this case, it is pitting home and family opposite to career, mother versus father, your needs and your community's needs. This lunar eclipse can be especially emotional. The eclipse might also ask you to choose between your love and a friend or between your company and your own happiness.

July 2, 2019: Total Solar Eclipse Cancer. This new moon marks a new beginning in your family life or emotional space. The key phrase here is "I feel!" Good time to start a family and make a move to a new location. The eclipse falls in your house of love and children. A great time to start a new creative project, to give birth to a new self, to get pregnant, or to fall in love.

July 16–17, 2019: Partial Lunar Eclipse Capricorn. This full moon in Capricorn again pits career versus home and family, mother figures versus father figures. You can see that this is a recurring theme of the year. In addition, it will once again ask you to balance your happiness, children, and love with your friends and organization.

December 26, 2019: Annular Solar Eclipse Capricorn. This new moon in Capricorn falls in your house of friends, altruism, and humanity. A great deal of action and new beginning even if it is the end of the year and holidays. The key phrase is "I Use." Try to use whatever resources you have to manifest new wishes and dreams in your life. It is another time when you can start a new company or join a new organization.

 ## Mercury Retrograde – Mental Landscape

During Mercury retrograde, it is not recommended to start new long-term projects, sign documents, make large purchases, get married, publish, start marketing campaigns, or release new products. Communications of all sorts are slower and filled with glitches and challenges. Computers crash, stock markets turn volatile; flights are delayed; traffic is worse than usual; accidents occur more often; and Murphy's Law takes hold of our lives. For example, the infamous Flash Crash of May 6, 2010, took place during Mercury retrograde in Taurus (the sign of money and the stock market). If you need to fly during Mercury retro, make sure you do your online check-in and take longer to reach the airport. Try to avoid overscheduling yourself or being overly critical and demanding. Also pay attention to your diet and food intake.

If you must start a new project, be as mindful as you can. Pay attention to small details and read in-between the lines if you must sign a document. Rewrite your emails, edit your texts, and think before you speak. In fact, it is better if you spend more time listening than talking. Life does not come to a halt during Mercury retrograde. You can still achieve a great deal. Mercury retro is like going on a vacation while it is raining. It is still possible but not much fun. However, it is a great time to edit, redo, reexamine yourself and your path, revisit old projects, and find lost objects. It is said that there are more coincidences and synchronicities while Mercury is retrograding. Try to focus on activities that have the prefix re – reevaluate, reedit, redo, reexamine, reconnect, regenerate, revisit, re-imagine, etc.

This year, Mercury is retrograding in water signs. Because you belong to the water clan, Mercury retro will not be as tough as last year. As a Water-Bender, you will be able to intuit and flow with the retrogrades, but don't get cocky or overconfident.

Between March 5 and March 28, Mercury retrogrades in your sign, Pisces, which falls in your first house of body and personality. People might not understand you too well. They might misinterpret your intentions. Please watch your body and health.

Between July 7 and July 31, Mercury retrogrades in Leo and then moves to Cancer, shifting the confusion from your house of work and health to your house of love and children. There could be miscommunication and misunderstanding with lovers, children, coworkers, or employees. Watch your diet and health. Not a good time for surgeries and medical tests.

Between October 31 and November 20, Mercury retrogrades in Scorpio in your house of travel, education, truth, and philosophies. Take extra care if you plan to travel abroad or work with multinational corporations. There could be issues with in-laws. Stay away from liars and people who steal your time or energy.

Unpredictability, Originality and a Touch of Chaos

In May 2018, Uranus moved into Taurus and will stay there until 2026, which falls in your house of communication and business. Please pay attention to how you talk, text, write, or market yourself or your products. On one hand, you might find yourself being funnier and more ingenious, but on the other hand, people might perceive you as rebellious or too crazy.

Uranus is called "the Joker" or "the Fool." It is chaotic but also brilliant. You might suddenly get an "aha" moment that can help your business, writing, networks, and communications. It is a great year to get deeper into social media and use new ways to deliver your message.

Due to Uranus' retrograde motion, he reentered Aries from November 7, 2018 and will stay there until March 6, 2019. This means that, for the first two months of the year, Uranus will be creating a bit more chaos in your finances and self-worth, but from March 6, Uranus is back where it will stay until 2026 and that is your house of communication.

Since Uranus is also in your house of relatives, siblings, roommates, and neighbors, it means that there could be some unpredictable chaos in your relationships with them. Use humor and friendship to dissolve any negativity with these people.

Uranus favors technology, innovation, and science. Maybe you can think of a great new application or an e-commerce business. It is also a good time to redo your website, give your Facebook page a face lift, and connect to social media.

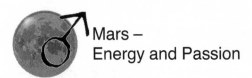 Mars –
Energy and Passion

Mars governs vegetation, action, leadership, passion, and aggression. In 2019, Mars will not be transiting in your sign; however, he will be traveling around your houses and projecting his martial influence through them. Below is a list of Mars' transits through the signs that can help you determine where to focus your energy. However, remember that even the best fighters need a general. Make sure you pace yourself and control your inner warrior.

 January 1 to Feb 14

You might feel aggressive but also powerful enough to manifest your wishes. This is a good time to exercise or find a new physical activity that can improve your health. This transit can help you make a push in your finances. It is a time to invest in your talents and express your gifts as well as stand up for your values. Be careful not to spend too much money or be impulsively generous to the wrong people.

 February 14 to March 31

This transit can help you boost your finances. It is a good time to invest in your talent and express your gifts as well as stand up for your values. Since Mars is transiting in your house of communication, you will receive and extra boost with your business, but your writing can be more aggressive. Be careful of fights with relatives, siblings, roommates, or neighbors. This is a good placement for sales and marketing. Uranus and Mars are coming together so be careful of accidents and mishaps.

 March 31 to May 16

Generally, this placement of Mars is good for winning arguments, and it can continue giving you extra energy in business and writing. Since Mars is in your house of home, it is a time to renovate your home, office, or workspace. This Mars location can cause unnecessary conflict with your family. Be extra careful of passive-aggressiveness or making others feel guilty. Actions and feelings need to connect.

 May 16 to July 1

A good time to continue renovation in your home if you have not started before. This Mars can also cause strife with family members. This Mars transit favors recreational activities, sports, hobbies, and fun. Love is in the air as well as creativity. Your inner child is active but be careful of injuries. If you have kids, they might create some conflicts and arguments. Since the North Node is in Cancer, you can use the dragon to fly you towards creative project and happiness.

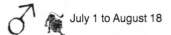 July 1 to August 18

It is also a wonderful time for recreational activities, sports, hobbies, and fun. You might feel a need to engage in risky endeavors so take heed with implosive behaviors. Love is in the air as well as creativity. This aspect can give you extra energy and passion in your work, as well as helping you find a new way to serve. A great time for diet and changes of routine. Be careful of arguments and fights with employees and coworkers. Be extra careful of injuries, inflammations, and stress.

August 18 to October 4

This time can continue giving you a boost in your work, service, and health. Mars is transiting in your house of relationships; therefore, it is great time for projects with partners. Be careful of lawsuits or conflict with enemies. This is a classic aspect of breakups. So be extra careful. It is also a time when you might embark on a crusade against your enemies.

 October 4 to November 19

Energy and flow continues with partners and relationships. Your significant others might start fights or cause movement in your life. Mars is transiting in your house of passion, sexuality, death, and intimacy. You will feel attractive and be able to attract opportunities in finance, investments, and production. Your own healing abilities can grow as well as the ability to help other people tap into their talents and finance.

  November 19 to January 2, 2020

This is a powerful transit for Mars as Mars is the ruler of Scorpio. You can connect your passion and sexuality or find a project that gives you a big drive. This transit of Mars falls in your house of travel and education. A great time for adventures and embarking on a journey to a place you have never visited either physically (traveling) or mentally (through study). It is a time to fight for your truth. Some conflict can take place with in-laws.

Venus: Money and Love

Venus is the ruler of pleasure, luxury, finance, talents, values, art, and relationships. She is also associated with Maat, the goddess of justice and law. Venus works in beauty cycles: the more you love yourself, the more you believe in yourself. The better your self-image, the more you connect to your talents. The more you develop and invest in your talents, the more money you can make. Venus' message is: love yourself and money will follow.

This year, the goddess of beauty will be in your sign between March 26 and April 20, making you more attractive, helping you get a raise, or tap into a new talent. It is a great time for romance, making money, and connecting to your artistic side. When Venus is in your sign, she is considered exalted and therefore far more influential. This is a good time for you to rebrand yourself, dress differently, change your hair, or get some new clothes. Not a bad time to indulge and pamper yourself (if it is healthy and does not harm you or anyone else).

Conclusion:

In 2019, you are making changes with your community, friends, companies, and affiliations. It is a year when you can make your wishes come true and help others manifest their dreams. Career and professional life will get a big boost and you will plant many seeds in your vocation and work. It is also a year to focus on love and children.

20358439R10119

Made in the USA
San Bernardino, CA
27 December 2018